DATE DUE

			PRINTED IN U.S.A.

GETTING YOUR GRANT

A How-To-Do-It Manual for Librarians

PEGGY BARBER
LINDA D. CROWE

*HOW-TO-DO-IT MANUALS
FOR LIBRARIES*

Number 28

NEAL-SCHUMAN PUBLISHERS, INC.
New York, London

Published by Neal-Schuman Publishers, Inc.
100 Varick Street
New York, NY 10013

Printed and bound in the United States of America

Library of Congress Cataloging-in-Publication Data

Barber, Peggy.
    Getting your grant : a how-to-do-it manual for librarians
/ Peggy Barber, Linda D. Crowe.
        p. cm. — (How-to-do-it manuals for libraries ; no. 28)
    Includes bibliographical references and index.
    ISBN 1-55570-038-1
    1. Library fund raising—United States.   2. Proposal writing in
library science.   I. Crowe, Linda.   II. Title.   III. Series.
Z683.2.U6B37   1992
025.1′1′0973—dc20   92-39145
                                                                                          CIP

CONTENTS

PREFACE

The purpose of *Getting Your Grant: A How-To-Do-It Manual for Librarians* is to demystify the grant process and to help public librarians get their share of the money available to them for interesting and innovative projects. It is aimed at staff of small to medium-sized libraries who may not be seeking grants because the procedures appear too cumbersome and time consuming.

There are many books that cover the topic completely, giving all the information you ever wanted and more. Too much information is often daunting and may in fact have kept you from attempting to develop a grant project.

Getting Your Grant is quick and easy. There are checklists and practical exercises to guide you step by step through grant development, plus large doses of encouragement. There are examples of proposals, fact sheets, and other materials that have worked well for other libraries. We have also interviewed funders and librarians to secure "real life" advice about what works.

We will take you through the process of getting your library ready to get a grant:

- Developing an innovative idea that will serve the mission of your library and interest potential funders;
- Identifying potential funding sources;
- Preparing your proposal;
- Following through—whether or not you get the grant
- Sources of further information.

Our focus is how to get grant support for library activities from government, corporations, and foundations. There are many other sources to help you plan a general fundraising campaign, direct mail appeals, and special events. For such plans we especially recommend James Swan's *Fundraising for the Small Public Library* (Neal-Schuman, 1990).

You are probably asking yourself—"Why bother?" You are already too busy. You and your staff are overworked, underpaid, and taken for granted. We are convinced grant seeking is a positive endeavor that can change your life, and help solve those problems. Here are a few of the reasons why:

1. To successfully seek grants you must be able to convincingly state your library's case. Developing your case statement is a healthy exercise requiring enthusiasm and fresh perspective. Every library needs enthusiasm and fresh perspective.

2. Grant seeking is outreach. It requires that you examine your services from a marketing perspective—from the point of view of the user. For example, you can stop worrying about how to make the community aware of the library, and start making the library aware of the community. Successful proposals are written with the users' benefit in mind.

3. Raising funds means raising friends. The contacts you make at each stage of the grant-seeking process can be new allies for your library. Most funders are not passive dispensers of cash, but partners in projects to improve the quality of life.

4. You have a head start and an advantage. Any book about grants will tell you that research is a major factor in developing successful projects. You are, by training and experience, a research expert.

5. Grant seeking gives you power. When you invest the time to develop a visionary project, you are in control of your library's destiny.

Getting Your Grant is a good idea. Try it!

ACKNOWLEDGMENTS

Our thanks to all the people who shared their advice about getting grants including: Tom Phelps, Barbara Will, Ruth Caine, Ned Himmel, Georgia Lomax, and Wicky Sleight. We thank Pat Read for her expert advice in the chapter on Foundation Funding, and for her guidance throughout this project. As the former director of publications and vice president of the Foundation Center, Pat has been the very best possible person to work with us, and the most patient too. Also thanks to our editor, Susan Holt, for helping us turn lots of pieces into a book.

Most of all, we're grateful for the opportunities our work has provided. Whether at the American Library Association or Peninsula South Bay Cooperative Library Systems, we can say as a team that being a librarian is not a job, it's a way of life—a wonderful way of life.

Peggy Barber
Linda Crowe

INTRODUCTION

What kind of projects get grant funds?

Grant support is ideal for one-time projects that will enhance future services. Grants are often given to launch new efforts that you can fund in the future from other sources. Funders rarely provide grant support for ongoing or existing services. Most foundation guidelines, for example, make it very clear that they do not fund operating expenses—so don't ask for grant funds to support your current staff or carry on business as usual. In brief, funders want to work with you to solve a problem or meet a need.

Funds are often granted for capital projects such as buildings or equipment. Grant funds for new buildings are useful to leverage other contributions, and can provide the large investment that will get a fundraising campaign off to a solid start.

According to The Foundation Center, public, academic, research, school, and special libraries received 1,091 foundation grants of $10,000 or more in 1989-90. These grants were made by 344 foundations and totaled $123,675,974. The list of the types of projects funded is headed by $41 million for buildings or renovation, $40 million for program development, $17 million for computer systems/equipment, $10 million for equipment, and $10 million for matching or challenge grants. But consider—foundations awarded total grants of *6.7 billion* in 1989. Libraries should be getting a bigger piece of the pie! Furthermore, private foundations are only one segment of the grant-giving community. In *Getting Your Grant* we will also examine strategies for securing federal and corporate grants.

Following are some examples of grant projects recently funded for public libraries:

The staff of the Young Adult Services Department of the Prince George's County (Maryland) Public Library received a $10,000 Library Services and Construction Act (LSCA) grant from the Department of Library Development and Services of the Maryland Department of Education in 1987-88. The Life Skills project developed materials and services to introduce young adults—especially teen parents and high school seniors going straight to entry level jobs—to the full range of services available at the library. (For a description of the project see *Public Libraries*, July/August 1990: 215-219.)

The Detroit Public Library received a grant of $257,763 from the W.K. Kellogg Foundation in the fall of 1990 to transform 6,788 Detroit Public School students into competent library

TEN COMMANDMENTS FOR SUCCESSFUL GRANTS

There are ten commandments for developing successful projects, and if you follow them and refer back to them you will have a clear road map for the process:

1. Develop a project that enhances the goals and objectives of the library.
2. Involve the staff in every step—developing an idea, funding strategy, the proposal, and its implementation.
3. Be sure the library has the basic resources to support the project.
4. Thoroughly research potential funders.
5. Confirm the interest of a potential funder before writing your proposal.
6. Consider the funder a partner in the project, not a silent source of money.
7. Write a proposal that is clear and concise, demonstrating vision and technical competence.
8. Prepare a budget that is detailed, comprehensive and realistic.
9. Be prepared to publicize the project when funded, during implementation, and when completed.
10. Build and maintain a relationship with the funding organization.

users. The three-year program is aimed at students in kindergarten and grades three, six, and eight. A recent study found that only 20 percent of the young people in the area were registered for library cards.

School Library Journal, November 1990: 15

The Newport Beach (California) Public Library received major help on a $7 million building campaign from the local Harry and Grace Steele Foundation. The foundation agreed to match other private gifts dollar for dollar, up to $500,000.

Library Journal, April 15, 1991: 16

In December 1989 the Atlanta Fulton County Public Library received a $400,000 challenge grant from the National Endowment for the Humanities. The grant, requiring a $1.2 million private sector match, will support intensive collection development for a new public, noncirculating, research library on the African-American experience.

Wilson Library Bulletin, February, 1990: 17

The Vienna (West Virginia) Public Library received a $5,000 grant from the Bell Atlantic/ALA Family Literacy Project for a program called CAPER (Children and Parents Enjoy Reading). Families with at least one child aged eight or under will participate in a program emphasizing tutoring for parents, training for parents in how to model reading behaviors, reading/activity session for children, and library skills sessions for families. Cooperating agencies include Literacy Volunteers of Mid-Ohio Valley, and Wesley United Methodist Church.

ALA News Release, September 1991

On August 5, 1992 the New York Public Library received a $1 million grant from the U.S. Small Business Administration to contribute to the design and engineering of its new Science, Industry and Business Library (SIBL), expected to open in 1995. The day it opens at the landmark B. Altman Building, the Science, Industry and Business Library will be the largest and most comprehensive public science and business library in the world.

NYPL news release, August 1992

In Plainview, Texas the James and Eva Mayer Foundation granted $15,000 to the Hale County Literacy Council (Unger Memorial Library) for creation of a literacy center as part of the library's meeting room, including computers and software for literacy students' use.

Newsletter of the Unger Memorial Library, July 1992

Getting Your Grant will show you how to get this kind of support for your library. Each chapter will take you through one or more steps. Use the checklists and worksheets to begin outlining your own plan. Don't just read this book—write in it. Get involved. Get going. Just do it!

1 GETTING READY

To receive a grant you must be able to convince a funding agency that your library is an excellent investment. Funders seek needy and worthy organizations—not the helpless, or hopeless. You must be focused about what you do and why you do it. You must be able to communicate how valuable the library is to the people it serves and communicate it in a way that is clear, well organized, impressive, and competitive. Think about it. If a local foundation receives 73 proposals prior to their annual board meeting, what will make yours worth a second look? Is your library presented as an effective and expertly managed organization that is indispensable to your community?

PLAN FIRST/FIRST PLAN

Getting ready to seek grants means planning. As you are undoubtedly aware, The Public Library Association (PLA) offers a collection of excellent tools to help librarians with the planning process. That process is based on three principles:

- Excellence must be defined locally—it results when library services match community needs, interests, and priorities.
- Excellence is possible for both small and large libraries—it is more of a function of commitment than of unlimited resources.
- Excellence is a moving target—even when achieved, excellence must continually be maintained.

Planning and Role Setting for Public Libraries, American Library Association, 1987

Successful planning begins with a sound evaluation of your community and its needs. What are your community's information needs? Are they being met now? By the library? By other organizations? What kind of role should your library play? These are just a few of the questions you must answer as you begin to plan.

First, define your mission. If your library has a mission statement, take a good hard look at it to see if it's still current and applicable. If your library doesn't have a mission statement, your very first job will be to create one.

Your next step is to set specific goals and objectives. Then develop a realistic schedule. Each of these steps will be discussed in more detail in the next several pages. The important point to remember is that regardless of whether you follow every hallowed step of the planning process, you have to plan. You have to be able to express the library's mission and to communicate effectively with your community.

The trick is focusing on the needs of the user, rather than library traditions and the status quo. The PLA planning process is "marketing" oriented. The marketing perspective is what you need for developing successful grant projects. It requires getting outside the building—getting the community involved.

Here are two of our favorite quotes about marketing—first a definition and then an application to libraries:

> Marketing is that function of the organization that can keep in constant touch with the organization's consumers, read their needs, develop products that meet these needs, and build a program of communications to express the organization's purposes.
>
> *Philip Kotler* and *Sidney Levy* "Broadening the Concept of Marketing," *Journal of Marketing.*
> January 1969

> It boils down to just two things. You've got to have accountability and you've got to have visibility. . . . We've got to satisfy our customers, and that may not mean protecting precious programs that only librarians like.
>
> *Lillian Bradshaw*
> Director, retired
> Dallas Public Library

The list of source materials in the Bibliography includes several recommended books on marketing and the planning process for libraries. Here is a brief summary of four basic steps in the marketing process:

1. Research and analysis

- Study the community—review the demographics (age, income, ethnic backgrounds, occupations, educational levels, religion, interests, community groups). You should be aware of trends in the demographic data. Much of this information is available from secondary sources such as census reports, city and county data books, or Chamber of Commerce reports.

- Evaluate the library's current status in the community. What do people think of the library? What is its public image?
- Assess needs. What are major target audiences? What are their needs? What is the present level of library success in meeting needs? Target audiences might include business people, students, parents, children, people who need literacy training, government officials, etc.
- Some libraries have embarked on extensive market surveys conducted by professional consultants to gather data about public needs and perceptions. If you don't have the benefit of such research you can conduct user surveys through questionnaires (Figure 1-1 shows one that was distributed with a local newspaper). You might also gather reports from other community groups, or interview leaders of key community organizations such as service groups, unions, churches, school and parent groups.

2. Planning

- Make the marketing program a part of the total library program. Using the research information, involve staff, board and community leaders in developing the library's mission goals and objectives. (There is more about developing a mission statement later in this chapter.)
- Plan programs and services to better serve the interests and needs identified in your research. Develop a strategy and timetable for reaching specific target audiences. Many librarians feel the pressure of trying to be all things to all people. A careful plan with focus on specific target groups does not mean you must refuse service to others. It does mean you have a strategy for making the best use of current resources, and plans for improving resources in the future.
- Seek allies for support of the library program. Develop a Friends group.

3. Communication

- Develop a basic library fact sheet (see Figures 1-2 through 1-4).

FIGURE 1-1   Community Survey Questionnaire

September 1987

Dear Neighbor:

In order to best serve you and our community, we are working with the American Library Association on a survey to learn more about what you want from the Platte County Public Library.

Please take a few minutes to fill out the survey. The results will be used to determine how our library can best meet your needs. Your responses are confidential and will be used only in combination with the responses of others.

Thank you so much for helping us with this important project. Please respond as soon as you can—October 1, if possible.

To return the questionnaire, just fold it so that the address is on the outside, tape it closed, and drop it in the mail. No postage is necessary. Thank you for your time and interest.

Sincerely,

Debby Hunkins
Jamie Wilhelm
Dave Burke
Platte County Library Board

For office use	Respondent # _____	(01-04)
	Branch _____	(05)
	Wheatland	–1
	Guernsey	–2
	Chugwater	–3
	Glendo	–4

1. Do you know the location of the public library in your community? (06)
   - yes ☒ –1
   - no ☐ –2

2. Do you have a library card in your own name? (07)
   - yes ☒ –1
   - no ☐ –2

3. Please "x" the box below that best describes *how often* you have telephoned or visited a branch of the Platte County Public Library *in the past year.* (08)
   - not at all in the past year ☐ –1
   - less than once a month ☐ –2
   - 1-3 times a month ☒ –3
   - once a week or more ☐ –4

4. If you have not visited or telephoned a branch of the Platte County Public Library in the past year, please "x" each box below that is a reason why you, personally, *have not visited or phoned* the library in the past year. (09)
   - Don't have time to go/call ☐ –1
   - Library hours are inconvenient ☐ –2
   - Parking is inconvenient ☐ –3
   - Library doesn't have the kinds of materials, services I need ☐ –4
   - I use another library ☐ –5
   - I'm not a reader ☐ –6
   - I don't need a library ☐ –7
   - Other (write in below) ☐ –8

   _____ (10)

   (If you have not used a branch of the Platte County Public Library in the past year, please skip to Question 8.)

5. Which branch of the Platte County Public Library do you use most frequently? Please "x" only one box. (11)
   - Wheatland ☒ –1
   - Guernsey ☐ –2
   - Chugwater ☐ –3
   - Glendo ☐ –4

6. Please "x" the box that best describes your most frequent purpose for using the Platte County Public Library. Please "x" only one box. (12)
   - For information or materials related to school ☐ –1
   - For information or materials related to job/career ☒ –2
   - For information related to personal interests or needs ☐ –3
   - To get reading materials for leisure time use ☐ –4
   - To get other materials for leisure time use ☐ –5

7. Are you generally satisfied with the hours, facilities, collections and services provided by the Platte County Public Library? (13)
   - yes ☒ –1
   - no ☐ –2

   Why do you feel that way? (14-16)

   _____
   _____
   _____

8. Below is a list of materials, programs and services that some libraries offer. In Column "A" please "x" the box beside each item that *you, personally,* feel the Public Library *should* offer. In Column "B", please "x" the box beside each item that you feel the Platte County Public Library *does offer.*

Materials	A. Libraries Should Offer (17)	B. Platte County Library Does Offer (20)
Paperback books	☐ –1	☒ –1
Records and audio cassettes	☐ –2	☒ –2
Films	☐ –3	☒ –3
Videocassettes of recent movies	☐ –4	☐ –4
Videocassettes on educational topics	☒ –5	☐ –5
Videocassettes on "self-help" topics (e.g., fitness, exercise, do-it-yourself projects)	☒ –6	☐ –6
A-V equipment (record players, cassette players, film projectors)	☐ –7	☒ –7
Magazines and newspapers for use in the library	☐ –7	☒ –7
Special books and magazines for business or professional people or other occupational groups	☐ –8	☒ –8

Programs	A. Libraries Should Offer (18)	B. Platte County Library Does Offer (21)
Programs for children, such as story hour, films	☐ –1	☒ –1
Films and lectures for adults	☐ –2	☐ –2
Programs for teens	☐ –3	☐ –3
Literacy programs (helping people learn to read)	☒ –4	☐ –4
Programs for senior citizens	☐ –5	☐ –5

Services	A. Libraries Should Offer (19)	B. Platte County Library Does Offer (22)
Assistance in finding materials or answers to questions	☐ –1	☒ –1
Answers to information questions over the phone	☐ –2	☒ –2
Out-of-library services for the homebound	☒ –3	☐ –3
Referral center to direct questions about community services to the appropriate agency	☐ –4	☐ –4
Inter-library loan system to get books not available at the Platte County Library	☐ –5	☒ –5

9. What, if any, services, materials or programs would you like to see Platte County Public Library offer or offer more of? (23-25)

   _____More____books____on tape_____

FIGURE 1-1   Community Survey Questionnaire, Cont.

Classification Questions

10. What is your age?   (26)

Under 18	☐	–1
18-24 years	☐	–2
25-34 years	☐	–3
35-44 years	☒	–4
45-54 years	☐	–5
55-64 years	☐	–6
65 years or older	☐	–7

11. What is the highest grade of school you
    have completed?   (27)

8 years or less	☐	–1
Some high school/trade school	☐	–2
Graduated from high school/ trade school	☐	–3
Attended college	☐	–4
Graduated from college	☒	–5
Graduate school	☐	–6

12. Including yourself, your spouse, your
    children, and any others living with you,
    how many people are there in your
    household? ("x" one box)   (28)

One	☐	–1	Five	☐	–5
Two	☐	–2	Six	☐	–6
Three	☐	–3	Seven	☒	–7
Four	☐	–4	Eight or more	☐	–8

13. How many children do you have living
    at home? ("x" one box)   (29)

None	☐	–1
One	☐	–2
Two	☐	–3
Three	☐	–4
Four	☐	–5
Five or more	☒	–6

14. Into which of the following categories
    does your total annual household
    income fall? ("x" one box)   (30)

Under $15,000	☐	–1
$15,000 - $24,999	☐	–2
$25,000 - $39,999	☐	–3
$40,000 or more	☒	–4

— — fold

Platte County **Public Library**

Branches in Glendo, Guernsey and Chugwater
904 Ninth Street   Wheatland, Wyoming 82201   307-322-2689

No postage
necessary
if mailed
in the
United States

Business Reply Mail

First Class Permit No. 6783   Chicago, Illinois 60611

Postage Will Be Paid By Addressee

American Library Association
PIO Platte County Library Survey
50 East Huron Street
Chicago, Illinois 60611

- Develop a press list. Include all available media such as newspapers, radio and TV stations, cable outlets, community group newsletters, church bulletins, in-house publications of schools and businesses.
- Get to know the people on your press list. Share your plans and problems. Ask for their help and advice. Be aware of their deadlines. Read, watch and listen—become familiar with what they do.
- Learn basic public relations techniques. See the Bibliography for recommended resources.
- Combine imagination with common sense to choose (or create) the most effective publicity.
- Participate in community activities. You should be a walking, talking, very consistent and highly visible advertisement for the library.

4. Evaluation

- Continue to measure response to the library and to take readings on its image.
- Continue the research phase by monitoring demographics and planning evaluation as a basic part of every targeted communications program.
- Monitor progress toward measurable objectives set in your planning phase.

DEVELOPING A MISSION STATEMENT

It is important to develop a clear mission statement and express it effectively. Susan Carpenter is a facilitator consultant who helps groups grapple with their mission statements. She gives the following reasons for having one.

A mission statement describes:

- Who you are
- What societal needs you exist to fill
- What you do as an institution to respond to these needs
- Who are the stakeholders and what you do to relate to them

- What is the library's philosophy
- What makes the library unique.

If you are still not convinced that your library needs a mission statement, then consider these reasons for having one:

A mission statement explains the purpose of the library, it can be used as both an assessment and a funding tool and provides a vision for the library.

When you state your library's case—mission—to a prospective funder, you make it clear that you are making a difference in people's lives.

Some examples

Here are some examples of public library mission statements, developed through the planning process. Any one of them could be used to effectively introduce the library to a potential funding agency.

The mission of the Iowa City Public Library is to enrich the lives of the people it serves by providing information necessary or useful for daily living, by fostering a learning environment for children, by providing resources for intellectual recreation and personal development, and by making resources and facilities available to community organizations.

Recognizing the cultural and linguistic diversity or our urban and rural communities, the staff of the Monterey County Free Libraries provides free access to information, educational and recreational materials, and lifelong learning opportunities.

The mission of the Saint Paul Public Library is to anticipate and respond to the community's need for information; to facilitate lifelong learning; to stimulate and nurture a desire to read in young people; to provide reading materials to meet the interests of all ages; and to enrich the quality of life in the community.

The South San Francisco Public Library is actively committed to providing the best possible combination of library materials and services to meet the informational, educational and recreational needs of our multicultural community, in a professional manner, with a human touch.

If you do not have a mission statement and need help formulating one you might consider hiring a facilitator to work with your staff, board, and community leaders. Your state librarian can probably recommend an experienced consultant. If you can't afford a consultant, there are other resources in the community. City personnel departments, nonprofit agencies, and volunteer centers have staff trained in facilitation who might be very willing to assist you with the process.

TELL THE LIBRARY'S STORY

When you have your act together and have developed a clear mission statement, it will be time to consider how to impress a funder to invest in your library. Here is where the planning time pays off. It gives you all the raw materials for impressive conversations and presentations. Here are some ideas and tools to help you take the first steps.

DEVELOPING A FACT SHEET

After your mission statement, a fact sheet is the most useful basic tool you'll need when you start seeking grants. A fact sheet isn't a brochure. It is a simple and straightforward description of your library. It should be limited to a single page of easy-to-read clusters of information. You can use your letterhead or press release letterhead. Avoid library jargon. Be brief. Typewriter copy is okay. You will need to update the fact sheet frequently, so it shouldn't be expensive to produce. A fact sheet is one of the most basic communication tools, and you will find it invaluable in describing your library to the media, visitors, new staff or board members, or new users.

There are no hard and fast rules about what should be on your fact sheet—beyond the name, address, and phone number of the library. Your goal is to select your most impressive facts and statistics and to organize them in a way that is clear and easy to read. If you can put the statistics in an interesting and memorable context—all the better.

Sample fact sheets are shown in Figures 1-2 through 1-4 followed by a worksheet to help you develop your own.

Make Your Statistics Interesting

For fact sheets, proposals, and presentations, it helps to have a supply of amazing facts. In most cases, a string of dry statistics will cause instant boredom or confusion. The numbers need to be described in terms of trends, translated or compared in a way that will catch attention.

Here are some of the quotable facts developed at ALA for use with the media. You are welcome to use them as is, or consider them inspiration for developing your own.

- Public libraries are the **most efficient of public services**—serving 66% of Americans with less than 1% of our tax dollars.
- There are **more public libraries than there are McDonald's restaurants**—a total of 15,481 including branches.
- Public libraries cost taxpayers **an average of $15.10 annually per capita**—less than dinner for two at a moderate restaurant.
- **More children** participate in library summer reading programs (approximately 700,000+) than play Little League baseball.
- Americans borrow more than **1.3 billion** items for business and personal use from public libraries each year—books and magazines, but also records, video and audio tapes, toys, games, computer software and more.
- In 25 years, federal funding for libraries totals **less than the cost of one aircraft carrier** (estimated at $3.5 billion).
- **Libraries save** business leaders, scientists, and engineers an estimated $19 billion a year in information resources.

COLLECT TESTIMONIALS FROM YOUR PATRONS

It really helps to have words of endorsement from satisfied customers to go along with the numbers. If you use evaluation forms at library programs, the last question should be open-ended so people can give you brief comments in their own words. Gather comments from children too. Clip comments from news stories. Collect quotes from famous people, including local leaders and celebrities. Ask for statements of endorsement and ask people if you can quote them.

FIGURE 1-2   A Sample Fact Sheet

Burlingame Public Library

...Serving your library needs since 1912

CHECK IT OUT!
Books, magazines, large type books, pamphlets, maps, telephone books, videocassettes, audiocassettes, compact disks, local history materials, computers, cameras, audio/visual equipment, and much more!!

ANSWERS!!
Staff on duty all hours the library is open to answer your reference questions and locate materials!!

FOR CHILDREN!!
Storyhours, toddler story times, read alouds, summer reading programs, special Saturday programs!!

RESERVE A BOOK!!
Our automated circulation system allows us to locate a book for you at our library, or any other public library in the county!!

TAKE A LOOK!!
The library maintains current event fliers, and brochures for classes, lectures, and educational opportunities in the community!!

FOR YOUR CONVENIENCE!!
Meeting rooms are available for community groups. Apple and IBM personal computers with printers are available for your use. Plus, microform reader/printers and coin-operated copy machines!!

SYSTEM COOPERATION!!
Burlingame is one of nine jurisdictions cooperation in the Peninsula Library automated circulation system. Library cards issued at any San Mateo County public library are good in any other!!

THE PAST...
The Burlingame Library was authorized in 1909 and dedicated in 1912. The present building was originally built in 1931, with additions in 1959 and 1971. The Easton Branch was opened in 1943 to serve northern Burlingame.

VOLUNTEERS!!
The Friends of the Library provides a unique opportunity for members of the public to volunteer their time for fund-raising, outreach to shut-ins, and program activities. The Friends sponsor two book sales a year, in May and October, as well as an on-going book sale in the Main Library lobby!!

Main Library
480 Primrose Road
Burlingame, CA 94010
Telephone:
Circulation: 341-1036
Reference: 342-1037
Children's: 342-1283
Audio/Visual: 342-1284

Main Hours:
Mon - Fri   9am - 9pm
Saturday   9am - 6pm
Sunday   1pm - 5pm

Easton Branch Library
1800 Easton Drive
Burlingame, CA 94010
Telephone: 347-1794

Branch Hours:
Mon - Fri   2pm - 6pm
Saturday   2pm - 5pm
Sunday   Closed

FIGURE 1-3 A Sample Fact Sheet

Queens Library facts...

The System: The Queens Borough Public Library is an autonomous Library System consisting of 59 Branches, a Central Library in Jamaica, and the Langston Hughes Community Library and Cultural Center.

Position: *Queens is the fifth largest Public Library System in the country in both circulation and number of Branches. It has 1,077,287 registered borrowers and is utilized by hundreds of persons who come to browse, study, and attend programs but do not borrow materials.

*With a 1984-85 circulation of nearly ten million, Queens Library has the HIGHEST CIRCULATION among the three City libraries and among libraries in New York State.

The Library is a pioneer in outreach services, such as those to new Americans, and has a verifiable history of leadership and innovation among public libraries nationwide.

Funding: 89% of the Library's funding is from the City of New York as allocated through the city's annual budget process. 10% comes from state monies. 1% from miscellaneous sources. The Langston Hughes Library has special funding.

Population Served: A general population of 1,891,325, and a land area of 109 square miles is served by the System. Since Queens is notable for its ethnic diversity, the Library offers a variety of special materials and services to more than 100 different nationalities. Its Central Library Adult Learning Center provides information, consultation and workshops on jobs and careers. Queens Library's Volunteers for Literacy provide instruction to English speaking adults who read below fifth grade level.

A growing business community makes high use of the business & technology collection which contains Investment Services, Law statutes and business directories. Queens also offers free on line database searches.

Size & Nature of Collection: The 60 Agencies offer a collection of over 4,054,601 items that serves all ages and interests. In addition to hard cover and paperback books, Queens Library offers newspapers, magazines, phono recordings, and videocasettes.

In-depth collections in special subject areas, more than 4,000 scholarly journals and popular magazines, *the New York Times* from 1851, and special magazine and newspaper indexes on microfiche can be found at the Central Library in Jamaica

Special Collections include the Long Island Division which is devoted to the study of the past, present and future development of the four counties of Long Island, with emphasis on history and genealogy and featuring a map collection and census materials.

History: In 1896 the Long Island City Public Library, a forerunner of our system, was chartered. In 1901, in order to help the city consolidate administration,seven existing independent libraries joined to form the Queens Borough Library. Thus Long Island City (Nelson) Library and its Branches (Steinway, Astoria) and Hollis, Queens Village, Richmond Hill and Ozone Park received a charter and funds to build seven (Carnegie) libraries. Flushing, first library in Queens (1858), and Poppenhusen, a new library joined shortly thereafter. In 1907, the rapidly growing library was incorporated as the Queens Borough Public Library, and administration offices, until now housed at Nelson, were established in Jamaica, the population center of Queens. A badly needed central building was erected in Jamaica, opened in 1930, later expanded in 1941. In 1966, the Central Building moved to its present site on 89-11 Merrick Boulevard.

Future: Queens Library begins its 90th year with a new Outreach Department, expanded services to older adults, five newly renovated branches, five new MAC funded Adult Learning Centers and a new "bookstore look" in which all branches offer materials in a "merchandising mode" that makes them readily accessible. As funding becomes available, the Library plans to expand its automated circulation system, strengthen its materials collection and increase services to special groups.

QUEENS BOROUGH PUBLIC LIBRARY, 89-11 Merrick Blvd., Jamaica, N.Y. 11432
For More Information Contact 718/990-0705.

FIGURE 1-4 A Sample Fact Sheet

THE FREE LIBRARY OF PHILADELPHIA
FACT SHEET

- 54 LIBRARIES SERVING NEIGHBORHOODS THROUGHOUT THE CITY.

- OVER 760,000 REGISTERED CARDHOLDERS (FEBRUARY 1991).

- ONE OF THE LARGEST PUBLIC LIBRARY SYTEMS IN THE UNITED STATES, WITH COLLECTIONS TOTALLING 9.6 MILLION ITEMS.

- IN 1989, MORE PEOPLE VISITED THE FREE LIBRARY (4.3 MILLION) THAN THE COMBINED ATTENDANCE AT PHILLIES, EAGLES, FLYERS AND 76ERS GAMES (3.8 MILLION).

- OVER 57,000 REFERENCE QUESTIONS ARE ANSWERED EACH WEEK (NEARLY 3 MILLION A YEAR).

- 5.1 MILLION BOOKS WERE BORROWED IN 1990.

- 307,000 PEOPLE ENJOYED 15,600 PUBLIC PROGRAMS PRESENTED AT THE FREE LIBRARY IN 1990.

- THE FREE LIBRARY'S READER DEVELOPMENT PROGRAM PROVIDES 245 AGENCIES IN THE AREA WITH BOOKS AND SPECIAL PUBLICATIONS, AT NO COST, TO TEACH READING SKILLS TO OVER 15,000 ILLITERATE ADULTS EACH YEAR.

- THE FREE LIBRARY HOLDS OVER 500,000 RECORDINGS, 1.1 MILLION GOVERNMENT DOCUMENTS, 1.3 MILLION MICROFORMS, THOUSANDS OF FILMS AND VIDEOCASSETTES AND 3,500 MAGAZINE AND NEWSPAPER TITLES.

WORKSHEET 1-1

BUILDING A FACT SHEET

1. Mission

2. Size of library:
   Collection:
      Books _____
      Recordings _____
      Videocassettes _____
      Magazine and newspaper titles _____
      Government documents _____
   Buildings _____
   Number of buildings or service outlets _____
   Staff _____
   Hours open per week _____

3. Number of borrowers _____
   Percent of population _____

4. Use
   Reference questions answered (week, month, year) _____
   Books borrowed _____
   Kids attending story hours _____
   Adults attending programs _____

5. Funding (not necessarily the amount, but sources of funding—translate community use and support into interesting statistics or comparisons such as annual expenditures per capita as compared to cost of one evening at the movies)

6. Special services or special projects

7. History (if it's fascinating, and if you can be brief)

8. Major trends or new directions

The Cromaine Library in Hartland, Michigan held a Super Patron contest and asked people to submit accounts of their library experiences. Here's just one example:

> Besides giving me many hours of enjoyment with your fine books and magazines, I have improved my learning and understanding through you. Cromaine has helped me to more important things than repairing tractors or building pole barns. Cromaine had helped me raise my children to give them feeling for their fellow human beings, their neighbors, their friends. Cromaine has helped in many ways from the use of the community room when our subdivision needed a place to meet, to helping with information on special projects. Most of all, though, it helped me and my neighbors raise our children intelligently.

Following is a sampling of quotes from diverse sources. Again, use them as you wish, or let them inspire you to collect your own.

> All you need in life is truth and beauty and you can find both at the libraries in Chicago.
>
> *Studs Terkel*

> An eight-year-old boy, credited with saving his great grand-mother's life with mouth-to-mouth resuscitation, said he learned the procedure by reading about it in a library book.
>
> From an AP story, *San Francisco Examiner*, 1/21/86

> Every writer knows that all books begin in the library, and if you're lucky—they end there.
>
> *Richard Peck*

I could not read five years ago. I walked into a library one day and I went up to a librarian and she was so understanding. It changed my life.

Diane Francis (student, Adult Learning Center,
Queens Borough Public Library)

We marched for the right to vote, we marched for the right to equal access, we marched for the right to open housing and now we'll march for the right to read.

Rev. Jesse L. Jackson

It won't matter that I set the NFL record if two years from now, if kids can't go the library and read in a book what I did.

Derrick Thomas

Defend your local library as if your freedom depended on it.

John Jakes

A library is just as important a part of our infrastructure as any road, bridge, public building or utility.

A. Drue Jennings
(President, Kansas City Power & Light Co.)

Certainly if America could be personified—it would be by more than 115,000 libraries—public, research, academic, school and others. . . . Librarians are the watchers on the walls of our civilization, fending off censors, and preserving the nation's culture.

Editorial, *Oklahoma Observer*

SHARING YOUR VISION

The style and substance of excellent public library service start at the top. The vision and stated mission of the library must belong to the director, but they also must be shared. Before you begin developing a grant project, it is important to consider how the activity will be received by your board, staff, and Friends, as well as by authorities such as the city manager, mayor, or town council. Only when all these local audiences have been involved in planning the library's mission and goals, *and* your development plans, will a grant proposal be feasible.

If you describe your great idea for a grant project will your staff recoil with horror, afraid that you are creating too much work? Will your board fear that the project will detract from basic library service? Will the Friends group feel left out and unimportant? Will the city manager think your tax support can be cut since you are raising outside funds?

If you answer *yes* to any of the above questions, there is still time to return to *go*, and start over. Rosabeth Moss Kanter, the Harvard management pro and author of *Changemasters*, describes leaders as being able to get people involved and inspired. She calls the process *tin-cupping*. The changemaster takes a brand new idea and presents it, like a tin cup, in one-on-one conversations. If you can capture peoples's interest and imagination, they will chip in. Your idea should relate to your mission and goals. The idea will improve as it is shaped by reaction, feedback, and early enthusiasm. If enough people are willing to drop a dime in the metaphorical cup, the project is likely to thrive.

Ruth Caine, program director at the Bell Atlantic Charitable Foundation (see interview in chapter 5), recently shared some of her wisdom about getting people involved. Her homily strikes us as words for managers to live by—especially managers who hope to develop successful grant projects!

- Tell me and I forget.
- Show me and I remember.
- Involve me and I understand.
- Inspire me and I commit.

GETTING YOUR 501(C)(3)

Most foundations and corporations will award grants only to organizations that have a 501(c)(3) tax exempt status with the Internal Revenue Service. If you don't have a letter certifying your status as a nonprofit organization, you will need to fill out forms 1023 and 872-C. The forms are available from the IRS. You may want to consult your library's attorney for help in this process.

Foundations may also routinely ask to see your annual report and/or a copy of your latest audited financial statement and/or your total budget for the current and previous year. If you don't have a formal annual report, just let them know it. In our experience, they are more interested in the financial statement, and it does not have to be submitted in an annual report format.

You may also be asked for a list of your board members with information on the professional affiliation of each member.

CASE STUDY 1: A MODEL PLAN

The Board of Trustees of the Free Library of Philadelphia adopted a comprehensive plan on January 8, 1991. The planning process and an impressive summary brochure were underwritten by the Free Library of Philadelphia Foundation. The content of the brochure, titled "You Have the Power to Affect the Lives of Over Four Million People," is a model for all public libraries.

The brochure outlines their mission, roles, and plans, and illustrates all with captivating quotes and photos of people who use the library. It's possible that a few librarians will look at the Free Library's beautiful brochure and say, "They spent too much." We're more inclined to say, "It's about time librarians stepped forward with pride to reflect the value of our libraries." Also, the brochure notes the "assistance and support" of writers, a printer, an advertising agency, and a design firm. It is important to invest in creating an effective message, but don't overlook the possibility of securing contributions of talent and services.

The Free Library of Philadelphia has to compete for funding with hundreds of worthy local causes and venerable institutions. They must tell a real and compelling story and let funders know they are effectively managed and ready to grow.

Here's a sample testimonial from the brochure:

"I didn't think I was going to make it."

Never having spent a day in school in her thirty-six years, Dee Gregory recently enrolled in the GED program at the Library for the Blind and Physically Handicapped.

When the course was over, not only had Dee passed the exam but she was nominated as the outstanding student of the nearby the Pennsylvania Department of Education.

"In other programs, it was hard to make a goal or even attempt one. At the Library, no one sees you in a wheelchair. Just somebody else coming to reach a goal."

Now registered at a community college, Dee has her sights set on a university education. "I'm a person who's climbing a mountain with no feet. And I'm almost up on top. Then I'm going to reach out and help other people come up the mountain—people who were going through the same things as me."

"I use the Library when I need a book or a tape or just to talk with a friend. Now I'm writing an essay on child abuse. I just want to get all the information I can.

"I'm hooked on this thing called caring. To me that's what the Library is all about."

The brochure concludes as follows:

The people and stories profiled on the preceding pages are proof that the Free Library changes lives. Yet their stories represent only a fraction of the countless individuals who have turned to us over the past 100 years and who continue to do so today.

The plan that has been presented in this booklet is designed to guide the Library through the coming five years and serve as a foundation as we enter the twenty-first century. Such long-range planning is critical for an institution as vital as the Free Library.

But thorough planning is not enough. In order for the Library to continue to serve as an asset for this city, it must receive the resources it needs to fulfill its mission. Only then will the future of our region—and that of the four million people who turn to the Free Library each year— be secure.

A copy of the Free Library's fact sheet from the brochure is shown in Figure 1-4. Their mission statement is as follows:

The mission of the Free Library of Philadelphia is to provide to all segments of the population of Philadelphia a comprehensive collection of recorded knowledge, ideas, artistic expression and information; to assure ease of access to these materials; and to provide programs to stimulate the awareness and use of these resources.

The ALA brochure "You Have the Power to Affect the Lives of Over Four Million People" includes the longrange service plan from the Free Library of Philadelphia and information on the organization of their planning process. The package is titled *When They Turn to Us: Serving Diversity* and is available for $20 from the ALA Customer Service Department, 800-545-2433.

WORKSHEET 1-2

GETTING READY CHECKLIST

1. Can you make a convincing case for the value of your library?

2. Have you collected a few amazingly good testimonials from your users?

3. Have you done any market research? Can you document the interests and needs of your community?

4. Does your library have a mission statement?

5. Do you have a 501 (c)(3) letter from the IRS? Do you have an audited financial statement?

6. Do you have an up-to-date basic fact sheet describing your library and its services?

7. Do staff, board, Friends and community leaders share your vision for excellent library service?

2 DEVELOPING THE IDEA

They all want a good idea. As you read the interviews with funders in chapters 4 and 5 you'll note they all agree on the "good idea" as the basis for a successful grant project. Your idea has to have local impact, and must help to carry out your library's mission, but there are some national trends that can help you get started.

Believe it or not, there are foundations, corporations, and government agencies eager to give money to your library. At the American Library Association we receive two or three calls a week from companies that want to work with us to reach local libraries. Most of our foundation grants have been developed because the foundation staff contacted us. Federal agencies such as the National Endowment for the Humanities are anxious to get more good proposals from libraries.

There are many reasons funders will give you money. Libraries are hot. The following list of opinions about why we're hot is ammunition you can use to develop your own ideas.

Literacy: Libraries are central to the literacy movement. Librarians are in a perfect position to provide leadership to local literacy efforts, coordinating the work of schools and volunteer groups. There has been considerable national attention to the need for literacy training.

Kids: Public libraries provide unique services to children. Even if you're trying to reposition your library beyond traditional children's services, don't throw the baby out with the bath water. One of our strongest talking points is service to kids. People care about children. Many adults cherish childhood memories of the library. What you may find tiresome and trite, may be your greatest appeal. That's why family literacy is perhaps the best thing we have going right now—*very hot*. Teachers teach children to read. Librarians teach children to love reading. We are a vital part of educational reform.

Culture: Public libraries are cultural centers—for all people. In many small communities we are the only cultural center. In big cities, we may be the only cultural institution without an admission fee. In this age of mass communications and franchising, there are very few opportunities for individuals to pursue personal interests or discuss ideas. Public librarians provide that opportunity. And we can tie into anything—science, religion, art, music, politics, history—from 0 through 999, we have it all.

Diversity: There is also strong current interest in our changing population and issues of cultural diversity. Librarians can be—and are—major players in providing the ideas and information to help people extend their knowledge and understanding of a multicultural society. The Rapid City (South Dakota) Public Library has a slogan that expresses this well: "Come to the Library . . . Come to an understanding." After all, our business is opening minds.

Community: We have little competition in our role of identifying and preserving what is unique about our communities, whether small town or inner-city neighborhood. We organize information about local community services and promote its availability. We preserve local history and promote its availability. These services are essential, interesting, and fundable.

Technology: In the information age, probably only the public library will make new technology accessible to all. Bringing new technology to the community is of interest to funders, if you can convince them of its value to the people you serve.

Prestige: The public library is respected and revered. More than many other organizations that are seeking funds, we have stability, history, clout, and a standing in the community. People know what public libraries are and they like them. Many grant seekers have to first establish their identity and credibility. We are several steps ahead.

BRAINSTORMING

Where do good ideas come from? There is no simple answer; rather there are many interesting questions. You might want to use some of these questions in a staff and/or board meeting to get everyone's creative juices flowing. Brainstorming is well-established as an effective technique for generating ideas. Use it to help develop some solid projects for grant applications.

- Are there areas of your mission statement that call for more and better service than you are currently providing?
- Has your market research—formal or informal—suggested needs of client groups that you are not meeting?

- What are people talking about? Are there local news stories or national news stories about problems that the library can help solve? What are the agendas of local service clubs? Consider education reform, literacy, the homeless, cultural diversity issues, teen health issues, AIDS. The national and local problem inventory is bound to shape the funding agendas of foundations and corporations. How and when do you want to get involved?
- What do you want to do? For whom? Why? Make a wish list of programs your library would offer if money were no object. Are there things your library desperately needs to improve basic services? (Projects that look beyond the library to community needs may be easier to get funded. It may be easier to raise money to launch a family literacy project than to automate the circulation system.) Pick a top priority from the list. What will you need to make it happen? Consider space, time, money, and skills.
- Are there opportunities you are missing? You or someone on your staff should be watching library literature for *RFPs*—requests for proposals. From ALA to LSCA to the Barbara Bush Foundation for Family Literacy, the state and national journals include frequent announcements of grant opportunities. In many cases the application procedures are painless. These opportunities may be a good match with your library's mission.

Once you have the glimmer of a brilliant idea and support for it from board members and staff, the following worksheet will help you give it form and muscle. These pages are meant to be written on, because when you have answered these questions, you will be well on your way to developing a proposal. Answer briefly in the space provided. Think it through—quickly—don't be intimidated.

WORKSHEET 2-1

ANALYZING YOUR NEEDS

Is there specific evidence of a problem? Is there data from newspaper articles, statistics? What documentation?

What will happen if nothing is done about the problem?

Who is affected by the problem? Is there a group—organized or not—that you can call on to help you understand the problem and develop solutions? (Any project is strengthened by involving the people you hope to serve.)

What organizations are already working to solve the problem? How will your project relate to existing projects? What partners can you recruit for your library project?

How does the problem relate to the library mission? How does solving the problem help reach the library's goals and objectives?

Why (how) is the library qualified to tackle this problem (need)?

How will your project idea help to solve the problem? What makes the project innovative or unique? Necessary? Timely? Significant? (These questions get to the specific strategies you will propose. At this stage it is best to have a general idea rather than a lot of details. You can refine and adjust when you are actually preparing to discuss the problem and project with a potential funder.)

Does the library have the resources to carry out the project? Will additional staff be required? How will the project affect current staff and services? (Answers to these questions are the first steps toward a project budget.)

Do staff, Friends, and trustees support the project? How will you sell the idea to those who were not directly involved in developing it?

Why do you need a grant to carry out the project? Could you carry out the project without a grant? What will happen when the grant funds are spent? Can you assure a funder that your library is committed to solving the problem?

How will you assess whether or not your project has reached its objectives or what the impact of your efforts has been?

The final question is not a question but a suggestion—try to explain your idea to a total stranger, or at least to someone outside the library. If you can describe the problem and your recommended solution with enthusiasm and conviction, you are well on the way to success!

CASE STUDY 2: REDWOOD CITY LIBRARY

AN IDEA THAT BECAME A PROJECT

Ned Himmel, Information Services Manager at the Redwood City (California) Library, answered our questions about how he developed a 1989 LSCA grant to fund *A Year in the Life: A Visual Time Capsule of Redwood City*. The goal was to videotape events and individuals with the intention of fostering pride in the cultural diversity of the city's changing population. His answers provide insight into the development of the grant project.

Q: *What was your reason for doing this project?*

A: To preserve history as it happens using a new technology—video.

Q: *Why was this time chosen?*

A: 1990 was the beginning of a new decade and it seemed like a good starting point.

Q: *How was this project related to the library's overall direction?*

A: Local history is a key component of library service, and our library has a staffed local history room.

Q: *How was staff involved in the development of the idea?*

A: The staff brainstormed service objectives relating to local history. The plan was discussed and refined with their input.

Q: *Were they supportive of it?*

A: Yes.

Q: *Why did you apply for a grant to support it?*

A: This was a new direction for our service. There was a need for more staff and equipment.

Q: *Did you have staff available to support it?*

A: Yes, our Local History Specialist is a half-time position.

Q: *How did you sell it to staff who weren't involved in developing it?*

A: I presented it at staff meetings and recruited volunteers for aspects of the project.

Q: *Can the library support related activities after the grant period?*

A: We can support some.

Q: *Did your project address or solve a specific problem?*

A: Yes, it brought out information that was truly representative of the times to get a picture of the city as a whole. Redwood City is changing rapidly and no one else is documenting the change.

Q: *What would have happened if nothing was done abut this need/problem?*

A: The status quo would continue, and there would be a future lack of good historical information on the 1990s.

Q: *How does the project fit into the library's mission, goals, and objectives?*

A: It fits in with the library as a reference center and as the institution committed to local history.

Q: *Does solving this problem/need enhance the library's goals?*

A: Yes, it is a stated objective in the city budget.

Another thing to consider carefully as you develop an idea is who is affected by it. We asked Ned Himmel to list each group and each individual to determine how they were affected. Here is his list:

Jeanne T., Local History Specialist—added hours and duties; coordination of all parts of project, major impact.

Ned H., Information Services Supervisor—additional supervision of Jeanne T., more meetings, more time, probably four hours a week.

Jane L., Library Director—more consultations with Ned and Jeanne; informing other city departments.

Archives Committee—additional processing of donated materials.

Staff Volunteers—adjustment of schedules to accommodate project.

Advisory Committee—time for meetings and phone or in-person consultations.

Sherren H., Library Secretary—more bills to pay and reports to process.

CASE STUDY 3: AMERICAN LIBRARY ASSOCIATION

GRANT FOR A LITERACY PROJECT

It may be helpful to trace how one of our ALA grant projects came to pass: the Bell Atlantic/ALA Family Literacy Project. In this instance, the funder came to us (in January 1989). The Bell Atlantic Charitable Foundation had begun to sponsor a book program on public television and wanted to develop a literacy project, but had no specific ideas. The ALA has a commitment to literacy programs as a goal of our strategic long range plan. We were also in need of a project to carry out our "access" goal.

In order to develop a project idea and a proposal, we invited several library leaders from the Bell Atlantic region (six mid-Atlantic states) to a brainstorming meeting hosted by the director of the D.C. Public Library. ALA covered the cost of the meeting. Participants included librarians who would be served by the project, staff from appropriate ALA offices and divisions, Bell Atlantic Foundation staff, and a D.C. literacy provider who works part time for the library.

What kind of literacy project would benefit the libraries of the mid-Atlantic region? The consensus was a family literacy project to be administered by ALA that would include grants to local libraries, training, and a family literacy fair to showcase materials and expert resources. The group focused on family literacy as an opportunity for librarians to build on their expertise in serving children in order to reach out to new audiences.

The ideas came from the people who then agreed to serve on the project's advisory committee. The Bell Atlantic staff was involved every step of the way, and suggested that a Bell Atlantic community representative be added to the local family literacy teams in each community receiving a grant.

Following the planning meeting, ALA staff developed a proposal, shared it with the planning group for comments, discussed drafts with Bell Atlantic, asked ALA divisions and units for their input, participation on the advisory board, and endorsement. A final proposal was presented to the ALA Executive Board for approval (after preliminary discussion with the ALA President, who had declared literacy to be a major priority).

Following ALA Board approval, the proposal was submitted to the Bell Atlantic Charitable Foundation, and was funded in July,

1989. Since then second and third grants have been funded, and a third is pending. Forty five communities in the Bell Atlantic region have received funding and training for family literacy projects, and ALA is seeking new partners to make the program available nationally. In October 1991 the project was honored with a Point of Light Award from President Bush.

As an example of idea development, the Bell Atlantic/ALA Family Literacy Project illustrates the value of involving the people to be served, developing a working partnership with the funder, and taking time to get all the relevant people involved. The idea was changed and rearranged each step of the way. The process was time consuming but ultimately very worthwhile.

REALITY CHECK

INTERVIEW WITH GEORGIA LOMAX

Does all the theory and opinion you've read so far make sense in the real world? We interviewed Georgia Lomax, Director of the Flathead County Library in Kalispell, Montana—a remote and beautiful corner of the real world. Her experience is practical, exciting and encouraging.

Q: *Your library has received several grants, can you give us a quick sketch of your library and community?*

A: We are a county library serving Flathead County, Montana. We cover 5,100 square miles, there is a lot of public land—a valley in the mountains. We serve a population of 60,000, and have four branches. The main industries are logging and tourism. We have 22 full-time employees, including 3.5 professional librarians. The main library in Kalispell is open 65 hours per week.

We actually serve anyone. Because we have so many part-time residents, so many seasonal workers in the parks in summer and ski resorts in winter, and just so darn many tourists all year round, we figure everyone is our user. We do not charge any nonresident fee, but let everyone have access and ability to borrow our materials. While we may lose a little revenue, we gain a lot of good will (and we rarely lose books to our "nonresidents").

(Other stats updated for FY91: circulation-per-capita, 7.1; number of times each person would have used the library during the year, 4.22; educational programs, 322; attendance, 5979, or 18.5 per program.)

Q: *What grants have you received?*

A: We have had many, including three LSCA grants, the MacArthur Foundation Library Video Classics (see application form in Appendix A), state Humanities Council grants, NEH grants from ALA (see Appendix D), community foundation grants, and we develop lots of projects with community groups.

The Eagles Auxiliary gives us from $100 to $200 each year for large print books or audiocassettes. ACOA (Adult Children of Alcoholics) gave us money for the Bradshaw tapes, a popular motivational series. I found out that the Youth Soccer League had a small library they were having trouble maintaining. They gave us the collection, and now give us money every year for more books or videos. All these deals help build our collection, but also bring new people into the library.

The Royer Foundation, a local foundation, gave us $1,000 every year for books on science and birds—until they ran out of money. After that relationship was established, we only had to send a one-page memo each year.

The Fred Meyer Foundation does a lot of projects with libraries, and gave us a four-year grant to do collection development in land use planning. That led to a good relationship with the County Planning Department. We cataloged their collection and gave them permanent loan of some of the more technical books we acquired with the grant.

We've even had grants to support our literacy program that were usually given only to schools. Through networking we convinced the donor that it made more sense to give the money to us than to set up a whole separate program.

Our latest excitement is the $22,000 donation from a local individual with a private foundation. It is to purchase a CD-ROM network with five stations, eight CD-ROM drives and software to fill those drives. Three terminals are for the public and two for staff! Wow!

Q: *How long have you been the director?*

A: Since June 1987.

Q: *Did the library get grants before you came?*

A: They received some. They have had LSCA Title II building grants, and the Royer Memorial money started before I came.

Q: *Have the grants had a positive benefit?*

A: Absolutely! There are two kinds of benefits—tangible and intangible. Obviously we receive money and materials, like the MacArthur videos. The intangible benefits are networking, connections in the community and beyond. Grants also help us get attention. Getting a grant is news, especially when it means we can provide a new service. I usually tell Rick when we have submitted a proposal. He's the local newspaper reporter who covers the library. He then calls every third week or so to see if it has been funded, and when—or if—it is, makes a big deal of it. People around here have come to expect success stories from the library.

Q: *How do you hear about the opportunities?*

A: We get notices from the state library. We get a lot of referrals. Other county or city employees run across something and think we might qualify, or are applying for something and think they may be able to add some book money into it for us. Also, we make a large effort at networking (what a buzz word, huh?), and it pays off. People from other agencies, businesses, etc., come up with ideas and opportunities. And I read the journals—and not just library journals.

Q: *What other journals?*

A: Oh lots. There's no pattern. I read widely and randomly. Community contacts also provide information, and I keep my eyes and ears open.

Q: *How do you find time to do all this?*

A: I just do it. You have to have the attitude that you can do it. It also gets easier when you've done it. In fact we use the same material over and over. We have one stock paragraph that describes the area and what we do (see Figure 2-1). If you find things that work—why not use them again? Proposals go to different funders, and even the same funder has different readers. Once you do it, it's not that time consuming. The computer really helps.

I see grant writing basically as a form of gambling. You're betting time spent in writing the grant and setting the stage that your project will pay off. If you don't give it a try, you won't get the jackpot.

Q: *Do you apply for a lot of grants that are not funded?*

A: Actually, very few aren't funded. We have received hundreds of thousands of dollars. We wrote a proposal for an automation grant that wasn't funded—all the grants went to big cities in the East. We lost another one we really didn't expect to get, but we wanted them to know we are interested. It was a LSCA Title II building grant—we weren't at the stage to submit a serious proposal (too much ground work still to lay) when the grants were due. We figured that they could turn us down and tell us what they

```
FIGURE 2-1  DESCRIPTION OF FLATHEAD LIBRARY
```

Flathead County has a population of 57,800 (7/1/86 census estimates) spread across an area nearly twice as large as the states of Rhode Island and Delaware combined. It is for the most part rural. Severe weather, poor roads, and geography keep residents confined to the local area for much of the year. Nearest educational centers are in Missoula, Montana, three hours drive south, and Spokane, Washington, two states away. The beauty and isolation of the rugged Flathead Valley has drawn many people seeking to escape the problems of busy cities, and those who wish to return to nature or a simpler lifestyle. The area's economy is primarily supported by the short tourism season and by logging, an industry that has faced severe problems recently. Many residents are employed only seasonally. In 1980, the unemployment rate for the county was 13 percent. It has continued to remain above state and national averages during this decade of closures and cutbacks for local employers. The Library provides service through five library outlets. It also serves Swan River Forest Camp (a residential corrections facility for men), Montana Veterans' Home, day care centers, and nursing and retirement homes. A homebound service is being developed. The Library circulated nearly seven items per capita in FY88, with statistics showing that each person in the county would have used the Library 1.3 times during that period. The Library provided 368 educational programs during FY88, which were attended by 7,231 community members (nearly 20 people per program).

wanted improved, give us a critique. We'd have more details and some good input from grant readers that we could use the next year when we would be ready to go.

One that really disappointed us was a proposal to the Montana Board of Crime Control for a project on teen substance abuse and suicide called LIFT—Lifesaving Information for Flathead Teens. And we sent off one goofy one to explore the idea of computer scanning maps. I don't think the world was ready for it, but I'll try anything!

Q: *How does your staff feel about your grant activity?*

A: The staff likes it. I have one person who especially likes the humanities grants. She loves to run the programs. They also really like the collection development projects. Usually I give the Request for Proposal to the staff and ask them, if we're to provide this service, how should we do it? We picture ourselves as the renegades of Montana. We're in a very remote location, but we do just as much as, or more than, some of the big guys. We think we're a little superior. We like to be unique and innovative.

Q: *Have your projects received good press coverage and good community support?*

A: Yes. But there are some pretty conservative people in our area who tend to see grants as a waste of the taxpayers' money. This has come up a lot, but never about the library. We figure this money is going to be spent by the government whether we apply or not, so we might as well apply and have a chance of it returning to our people rather than having it all go some place else. We work really hard to be accountable and to provide a service people value.

Q: *Have you done the public library planning process? Do you have a mission statement?*

A: We haven't done the planning process. We have the books, but we've been getting grants instead! In our goals each year, we include the planning process, but we haven't gotten to it yet. Actually, we use the forms a lot. I guess we have done it—but in our own way. We have a mission statement, and we do use it in proposals (see Figure 2-2). It is very broad—could probably use more work. Our annual goals help give us ideas for grant projects. For example, we would like to start service for the homebound.

FIGURE 2-2   FLATHEAD MISSION STATEMENT

The purpose of the Flathead County Library is to provide access to information that will assist the public to:

- Pursue lifelong educational development;
- Become better citizens;
- Develop individual potential;
- Appreciate and enjoy works of art and literature;
- Enhance use of leisure time;
- Investigate and contribute to the growth of knowledge and
- Examine the original, sometimes unorthodox and critical, ideas necessary to a society that depends on free expression and competition in ideas and for its survival.

Library service is provided for residents of the tax district at the main library and at service outlets throughout the county as established, supported or discontinued by decision of the Library Board.

Q: *Are all your grants "off budget"?*

A: Yes, we don't include grant funds in our budget, and the county business department sets up a separate fund for each grant. This helps us keep track of each grant project for reporting.

Q: *Do you think getting grants has, or might, endanger the support provided by the county?*

A: Absolutely not, although this is always a concern for anyone funded by a government. We have a great working relationship with our county. They understand and support our efforts to seek *additional* funding—not *alternative* funding. They strongly support the idea that libraries are to be supported by the community, and if we are able to provide service or materials above and beyond local funding by obtaining more money, we're entitled to it. We keep our officials up to date on our projects, wish lists, etc., and they support us. I think they probably appreciate the attention and kudos we receive from the media, and which in turn reflects well on them. We really appreciate their cooperative attitude.

Q: *What is the most difficult thing about applying for grants?*

A: For some people it's getting the ideas. We keep a folder of ideas and things we want to do. It can also be hard doing it "their way"—remembering you have to fit into funders' goals. Sometimes the LSCA types can get really bureaucratic, but you have to put up with it.

Q: *What is your advice to librarians who have never applied for a grant?*

A: Just do it! Don't just think about it. Do it! Start with a little one. Ask the state library people for help. They can really be very helpful. The state humanities council will be glad to help too. Don't assume that the people you're applying to understand anything. And if you get turned down, don't worry about it. I guess it's also important to remember that grants can be political. You may lose an LSCA grant because of some legislator's influence, not because of the quality of your project. Just do it—just keep doing it.

3 IDENTIFYING FUNDING SOURCES

All nonprofits interested in attracting foundation funding should learn as much as possible about the funders in their own backyard, both large and small.

Foundation Fundamentals, 1991

There are three major categories of funders. Each requires a different approach.

GOVERNMENT FUNDS

Funds may be available from all levels of government: federal, state, county, and city. Although each may have very specific requirements, there are some general guidelines that apply across the board:

- Government grants usually have specific application forms and procedures.
- Since government funding carries out legislation, there are bound to be frequent changes in rules and regulations. It is important to call the agency in question before applying to make sure you have up-to-date information and the program is still in existence.
- Government grants usually have strict reporting requirements; careful record keeping is essential.
- The two most familiar sources for federal funding for libraries are the Library Services and Construction Act (LSCA) and the National Endowment for the Humanities (NEH). Call your state library for information about LSCA funds. For information about NEH funds, call your State Humanities Council (see Appendix C for a complete list), or call Tom Phelps, Humanities Projects in Libraries, National Endowment for the Humanities, Old Post Office, 1100 Pennsylvania Ave., N.W., Washington, DC, 20506. 202-606-8271.

There are other federal grant programs to which libraries may apply. For a current list the best source is the Catalog of Federal Domestic Assistance.

Government grants checklist:

- Check the Catalog of Federal Domestic Assistance for programs that match your project objectives.
- Check state, county, and local government agencies for relevant programs.
- Contact the state library agency for guidance and/or contact program officers at other agencies you have identified in your search.
- Talk with librarians or other organization staff who have received government grants from the agencies you have in mind.

FOUNDATIONS

Foundations are nonprofit organizations that expend funds to maintain or aid charitable, educational, religious or other activities serving the public good, primarily by making grants to other nonprofit organizations. The four basic types of foundations, each with different kinds of operations, are independent foundations, corporate foundations, operating foundations, and community foundations. Public information on foundation giving is readily available primarily through Foundation Center libraries. The Center and the distinctions among the different types of foundations are described more fully in chapter 5.

What all foundations have in common is that they must submit an IRS 990-PF tax return to the government. These documents are public record and are the basic source for the Foundation Center's information about foundation operations, assets, and funding history. The Center collects additional information to verify and expand the tax returns and has extensive databases to make all this information of maximum use to the grant seeker. We especially recommend *The Foundation Center's User-Friendly Guide: Grantseeker's Guide to Resources*.

Foundation Grants Checklist:

- Get to know the materials and services of the Foundation Center Libraries.
- Contact program officers at foundations to ask specific questions of update information available in Foundation Center directories.
- Talk with project directors at organizations that have received grants from the foundation you are targeting.

CORPORATIONS

In addition to corporate foundations, many companies have corporate giving programs. Information on corporate giving is not publicly available, but often corporations will make in-kind gifts of materials, facilities, and staff expertise—in addition to monetary contributions. Many will match employee contributions or provide release time for skilled staff members to use their talents working for a worthy organization. A library planning to install or upgrade computer systems might well consider applying to a local corporation for skilled consultants.

Since there are likely to be fewer standardized procedures, you can approach corporations with creative strategies. The most important point to remember is that corporate giving is almost always directly related to the benefit of employees and their families in the communities where the company conducts business.

When approaching a corporation, always keep the funder's self-interest in mind. A proposal to a corporation should emphasize how the project will help them achieve company goals.

Corporate Grants Checklist

- Use the services of the Foundation Center Libraries, including the *National Directory of Corporate Giving*, a biennial directory of direct corporate giving and corporate foundation activity.
- Read the business pages of your local newspaper(s) for reports of corporate giving activity.
- Contact the public relations staff of corporations you think may be interested in your library's project. Ask your staff and board members and the library Friends if they have corporate contacts, or if they know of corporate giving programs.

OTHER SOURCES OF IDEAS

When you begin to think about getting your grant, do not limit your thinking. Keep your eyes and ears open. Talk to people. Read. For a constant source of ideas, read the news sections of library journals, especially *American Libraries, Library Journal, Wilson Library Bulletin*, and *The Bottom Line*. You will frequently see announcements of grants to libraries and RFPs.

4 GOVERNMENT FUNDING

FEDERAL GRANTS: LSCA

Federal grants given through state libraries are the ones that public libraries are most familiar with, specifically Library Services and Construction Act (LSCA) Title I, II, and III. Title I is available for public libraries, public library systems, and institutional libraries. Title III is for all types of libraries, but is predicated on cooperation. Projects must benefit more than one type of library.

Title II is for construction and renovation of facilities. Since *Getting Your Grant* is concerned with program grants we again refer you to *Fundraising for the Small Public Library*, by James Swan, which covers Title II in detail. If it's a facelift you're seeking, see Swan.

LSCA Titles IV, V, and VI are also available directly from the federal government. Title IV is for Library Services for Native Americans and Hawaiian Americans; Title V for Foreign Language Acquisition Programs; and Title VI for Library Literacy. These guidelines are available from the U.S. Department of Education, Office of Educational Research and Improvement, 555 New Jersey Ave., N.W., Washington, DC 20208-5571.

Title I is the kind of LSCA grant most sought after by public libraries. It provides seed money for new projects, to develop models, or to add an innovation to an already successful program. The funds are not meant to be used for ongoing operations; however, the library is required to commit to the ongoing operation of the program after the grant funding ends.

All states have different LSCA processes and regulations, but they are still governed by federal legislation. That leads to our first tip:

GET THE LSCA HANDBOOK FROM YOUR STATE LIBRARY!

It will tell you everything you need to know about writing an LSCA proposal. The handbook or guidelines will tell you what kind of proposals the State Library is interested in funding. In California, for example, LSCA priorities include:

• Bringing library service to areas and to populations without services

- Improving library service to areas and populations with inadequate services
- Providing library service to disadvantaged persons, which includes low income, English-speaking minority cultures—such as African-American and Native-American groups—and other least-served populations
- Providing library service to physically handicapped persons
- Providing library service to persons in state institutions
- Supporting Major Urban Resource Libraries
- Supporting National or Regional Resource Centers
- Providing library service to persons of limited English-speaking ability
- Providing services to the elderly
- Providing Community Information Referral Centers
- Providing literacy programs
- Providing intergenerational library programs
- Providing childcare center library programs
- Providing library literacy centers
- Providing drug abuse prevention programs

All of these examples are listed in the *State of California LSCA Handbook* for 1990/91, and all fall within the federal LSCA guidelines. Surely, your project will fall into one of these categories.

In California, and some other states, an intent proposal is required. This is usually limited to no more than one or two pages and asks you to briefly describe what you want to do and what the estimated budget will be. (See Figure 4-1.) Your job is to entice the consultant at the state library with your idea. In fact, before you write one word you should contact a friendly consultant at the state library and tell them what you are thinking about submitting. They may encourage, discourage, or give you valuable direction on your project. Usually there is one consultant on the state library staff who is responsible for the area in which you are developing your project. Find out who it is and call.

Remember that before you write the intent letter you must consult with the people in your library who will be involved in the project and be sure they are ready to sign on to it. State library consultants have an uncanny ability to know whether the project is locally supported.

If your letter of intent sufficiently intrigues the state library staff, the LSCA advisory committee, and the State Librarian you will be asked to develop a full proposal (see Appendix B for an example). When you receive this letter there are often suggestions to incorpo-

FIGURE 4-1   Sample Intent Proposal

California State Library
Library Services and Construction Act
Fiscal Year 1991/92
Title I and III

PROPOSAL

Submit in four copies by 5 pm, **January 25, 1991** to Attn: Collin Clark, Library Development Services, 1001 Sixth St., Suite 300, Sacramento, CA 95814-3324.

1. Project title: __Staff Training Curriculum for a Multicultural Environment__

2. Applicant jurisdiction: __Peninsula Library System__

3. Address __25 Tower Road, San Mateo__   ZIP+4   __94402-4000__

4. Applicant contact: __Linda Crowe__   Phone: __(415) 349-5538__

5. Type of library: System __x__ , Public _____ , Academic _____ , Special _____ ,

   State agency _____ , Federal agency _____ , School _____ .

6. Population: Client __43,750__   Total __406,900__

7. LSCA Program Activity __disadvantaged persons__

8. Participants:

   Daly City Library
   Redwood City Library
   Santa Clara County Library - Milpitas Community Library
   Santa Clara Public Library
   Sunnyvale Public Library

9. LSCA amount requested: __$71,325__

Advisory Council Use

FIGURE 4-1   Sample Intent Proposal, Cont.

Project Title __Staff Training Curriculum for a Multicultural__
_____Environment

Jurisdiction ___Peninsula Library System_____

9. Project Summary: complete in the space provided.

> The Rand Study commissioned by the California State Library reports that, "In 1988 40% of the State's population was composed of several minority groups." It also states, "that there are fewer minorities among public library users and the general population." Libraries need to meet the challenge of serving diverse population groups, but staff often lacks the knowledge and tools to interact effectively with these diverse and growing groups. The specific goal of the project is to train public service staff to work effectively with the various multicultural, multiethnic, multilingual population in their communities.
> The objectives are:
> 1. To select an advisory committee of librarians representing 5 participating libraries and the target populations: Daly City, Filipino; Redwood City, Hispanic; Santa Clara County, Milpitas Community Library, Vietnamese; Santa Clara Public Library, Korean; and Sunnyvale Public Library, Chinese.
> 2. To engage a cultural broker from the target population to work with each participating library   November - December 1991
> 3. To develop a resource manual for training public service staff in both practical skills and behavioral techniques January - April, 1992
> 4. To train public service staff in participating libraries in practical skills and behavioral techniques developed for the project May - August, 1992
> 5. To test the skills developed during training in the resource libraries August - September, 1992
> 6. To evaluate the training techniques and the integration of skills into staff behavior   September, 1992 - ongoing
> This project has aspects of two statewide projects, but differs in significant ways. It builds on the concept of CORE training, to enhance staff confidence. Core relates specifically to reference skills, while this project develops staff confidence and competence to work with patrons from varied multicultural, multiethnic and multilingual backgrounds. The project focuses on cultural diversity as does Partnerships for Change. PFC emphasizes outreach to the community while this project looks inward at public service staff. However, the tools developed from the PFC process will be valuable resources for this project. If libraries are to reach all of the people in the community, staff must be ready to provide them with the services they seek.

10. Budget Summary:

	LSCA (1)	Other funds (2)	In-kind (3)	Total (4)
a. Salaries & Benefits	35,542		19,467	55,009
b. Library Materials	500			500
c. Operation	30,000		5,000	35,000
d. Equipment	0			
e. Indirect Cost	5,283			5,283
f. Total	71,325		24,467	95,792

11. Signature _Linda D. Wood_____   Date _1-24-91_

rate into the full proposal and a consultant is usually assigned to help you develop it. If you have been talking to the right person, the consultant will probably be the one who worked with you on the intent letter. You should be in regular contact with this consultant and send your working drafts to him or her. If the consultant is involved and likes the proposal you have a friend on your side when proposals are being evaluated. A cautionary word! Just because you are encouraged to develop a proposal from your intent letter this in no way implies that you will receive funding for the full proposal.

The application requires fleshing out from one page into several. You must state client needs and project goals, measurable objectives to reach goals, project actions in time sequence, personnel and staff training, statewide significance, the evaluation process and methods of continuation. You will also need to have a detailed budget and show in-kind contribution from the library. A one-page summary may also be required.

When your application is in final draft form be sure your consultant gives it a thorough reading. This is your last chance to make changes. As you develop the full proposal, be sure that appropriate staff members are involved and have a chance to respond to the drafts. If there is a project advisory committee they should meet and also contribute to the process.

Once the full proposal is submitted you will need to wait patiently for the answer, but you must be ready to react quickly if the answer is yes! You have only a year to complete this project so be ready to begin as soon as you receive word that you are funded. This is just the beginning. State library staff will remember not only how well you write a proposal, but how successfully you implement it.

If you are not funded ask your state library consultant why. Maybe it just wasn't the year for this project. Maybe it will work next year. This was the case with the project in Appendix B—it was turned down in 1990-91 but funded in 1991-92, and 1992-93. Don't give up if you really believe in it. Perhaps there are other ways and resources to try.

INTERVIEW

BARBARA WILL, LSCA

Barbara Will is the LSCA coordinator for the California State Library. She kindly agreed to share her experience by answering questions that shed light on the LSCA process. Although each state determines its own procedures within the context of state and federal law, the general guidelines apply in most areas.

Q: *What kind of application do you require?*

A: The California State Library has guidelines for the letter of intent (preproposal) and the proposal.

Q: *What kind of restrictions do you place on applicants and applications?*

A: Title I proposals are limited to public libraries and public library systems; Title II grants are for public libraries only; and Title III grants are for more than one type of library and/or system.

Q: *How many times a year do you consider applications?*

A: Generally once a year.

Q: *Is it a good idea to contact you or someone else on the development staff before a proposal is developed?*

A: Yes, that is always a good procedure to follow and in fact we encourage people with good ideas to submit proposals as well as try to make the proposals better.

Q: *Since grants under a certain amount may require less work, are there different procedures for approval?*

A: No.

Q: *Describe the grant evaluation process and should applicants be aware of this process?*

A: First, a letter of intent is received and it is reviewed internally by staff, and the LSCA Advisory Committee. The State Librarian reviews all recommendations and decides which preproposals are competitive and should be developed as full grant applications. When the full proposals are developed, the staff again reviews them and makes recommendations to the State Librarian who makes the final decisions. We hope every applicant understands that projects are carefully evaluated.

Q: *If the state library has a grant idea will you approach a library with a strong track record for successful projects to develop it?*

A: Rarely. It might be developed as a staff proposal.

Q: *What advice would you give a library interested in developing an LSCA proposal and when should a library apply for one?*

A: A library interested in applying for an LSCA grant should read the LSCA goals and objectives and decide if their project fits within those goals and objectives. It is also helpful to be aware of the major categories that the state library is interested in funding.

Q: *And what are those?*

A: At this time we are especially interested in meeting the multicultural needs of California's diverse population and in networking resources.

Q: *Do you assign a particular person at your agency to work with each proposal?*

A: Yes, we try to assign each proposal to a consultant who has a particular interest or expertise in the area addressed by the proposal. An example would be assigning a networking proposal to me because I am the network consultant.

Q: *Do you suggest programs you have funded to help applicants?*

A: No.

Q: *Is it advantageous to send your proposal early?*

A: No.

Q: *Will you visit a library or agency submitting a proposal to gain a greater understanding of the organization?*

A: No. The full proposal should be sufficiently complete to stand on its own.

Q: *Is it appropriate to send additional information between the filing date and decision date?*

A: In general, no. The proposal should be sufficient, but if circumstances change we would appreciate that information.

Q: *If you reject a proposal will you give general advice on how to improve the library's chances in the future?*

A: We always send comments and we are glad to talk to the proposal writer and discuss why the proposal wasn't funded or how it could have been more competitive.

Q: *What are common mistakes?*

A: Failure to follow instructions, insufficient information, and/or the proposal doesn't match the California State Library's or LSCA's priorities.

Q: *What are the elements of a quality proposal and what do you look for when you evaluate one?*

A: The elements of a quality proposal include a needs assessment, clear goals and objectives, clearly stated activities, a realistic timeline and a reasonable budget. I look for all of those things as well as evidence of careful planning, contributions to the statewide effort, and evidence that the project can be maintained after the funding period.

Q: *LSCA proposals are considered a great deal of work (although not as much as an NEH proposal). Is this true? How can you help?*

A: Yes, it does take work and planning to develop an LSCA proposal. State library staff can help by reviewing drafts and making helpful suggestions. At times we have been able to simplify procedures for smaller grants or special grants.

Q: *Last, but not least, what are the chances of receiving an LSCA grant?*

A: We fund approximately one out of every three proposals.

FEDERAL GRANTS: NEH

Democracy demands wisdom and vision in its citizens.

National Foundation on the Arts and the
Humanities Act of 1965

The National Endowment for the Humanities (NEH) is an independent grant-making agency established by Congress in 1965 to support research, education, and public projects in the humanities.

What do we mean by humanities? The legislation defines the humanities as the study of the following disciplines:

- History
- Philosophy
- Languages
- Linguistics
- Literature
- Archaeology
- Jurisprudence
- The history, theory, and criticism of the arts
- Ethics
- Comparative religion, and
- Those aspects of the social sciences that employ historical or philosophical approaches.

But anything may fall within the definition of humanities depending on how you examine it. For example, scientists can analyze the physical properties of the stars, but humanists can convert them to poetry and metaphor that illuminate human experience on earth.

The Endowment supports work in the humanities through programs administered by six divisions:

- Education Programs
- Fellowships and Seminars
- Preservation and Access
- Public Programs
- Research Programs
- State Programs.

In addition, there is one office—Challenge Grants.

Getting Your Grant will focus primarily on Public Programs. NEH sees libraries as parallel schools that can provide the general public with resources, guidance, and a natural setting for study of the humanities. Funding is provided for a variety of formats such as reading and discussion programs, lecture series, conferences, film and discussion groups, and exhibitions.

In 1991 NEH made grants totalling $2,973,000 for public programs in libraries. The largest grant was $305,679 the smallest was a planning grant for $21,260. Sixty nine applications were received and 25 grants awarded—more than one third. The average grant size is $114,000.

Think about all the problems facing our nation today, and think about what we as librarians can do to help people find understanding and solutions. We really can! Humanities programs in libraries help people to know and to understand. Librarians from across the United States report that programs on literature, ethics, popular fiction, history, other cultures, art history, and poetry are bringing men and women to the library in record numbers. The library is one of the few public places where adults can get together to exchange idea and experiences. As one participant in a discussion program said, "I'm surprised at what I hear myself saying. I never thought I had these things stored up inside me. But I do."

Two choice bits of advice if you seek NEH grants:

1. Work with the NEH staff on developing your idea.
2. Involve a humanities scholar every step of the way. Appropriate credentials are essential—a Ph.D. in one of the disciplines of the humanities; a track record of research and publication; or a teaching position in the humanities in a college or university. Some state humanities councils and state library associations have directories of scholars who have worked with libraries. ALA has a directory of scholars, or you can contact a local college or university.

Write or call NEH for *Humanities Projects in Libraries and Archives; Guidelines and Application Instructions*, but don't be daunted by this publication. It is actually very helpful, but the staff is even more helpful. (See the interview with Tom Phelps that follows.) Many rumors have circulated about how impossible it is to apply to NEH. Not true! A substantive and well-planned proposal is required, but the chances for funding are good, and well worth the effort.

OTHER SOURCES

The state humanities councils are also good sources of assistance and funding for library programs. (See the list of state councils in Appendix C.) You might also contact your state arts council. While most arts councils haven't as frequently provided funds to libraries, many support authors on tour and will subsidize author appearances in libraries. Traveling exhibitions may also be available from arts councils.

The American Library Association has a tradition of NEH funded humanities programs, including the very visible "Let's Talk About It" reading and discussion programs that have become a tradition in hundreds of public libraries. The ALA also administers traveling exhibitions in partnership with institutions, such as the New York Public Library or Smithsonian, that develop major interpretative exhibits.

The ALA programs are frequently demonstration projects, providing materials, training, and funding for local library programs. The process of applying to ALA for a humanities program is usually very simple; a sample application form is reproduced in Appendix D. ALA announces NEH program opportunities through news releases to the national and state library press, state libraries, and state humanities councils. For more information on ALA humanities programs, contact Deborah Robertson, Director of Public Programs, 800-545-2433 ext. 5057, or write to her at ALA, 50 East Huron, Chicago, IL 60611.

The National Endowment for the Humanities also has a challenge grant program that can provide funds for endowments designed to build humanities collections or programs, capital projects, preservation, or special programs in the humanities. The NEH funds must be matched three to one on an initial challenge grant. The challenge becomes a great way to leverage other non-federal contributions. These funds are not just for large libraries. For more information write to NEH for the challenge grant guidelines, and ask to see sample proposals.

INTERVIEW

TOM PHELPS, NEH

Tom Phelps, Director of the Humanities Programs in Libraries and Archives at the National Endowment for the Humanities in Washington, D.C., is a librarian. His job is to help us—librarians across the nation—develop humanities programs in libraries. He is a wonderful and supportive resource. We urge you to write or call him for sound advice on developing humanities programs in your library. He will tell you if your project idea has a better chance at the state or national level, and will give you straight information on any aspect of NEH funding for libraries, whether you are seeking a challenge grant, funds for preservation, or for programming.

Tom Phelps is our guide and guru in Washington, and he was typically generous in giving his time for this interview about how to develop successful humanities program proposals and how to get them funded.

Q: *What is your advice to librarians from small or medium sized public libraries who are interested in launching humanities programs?*

A: I suggest they first apply for the NEH projects that the American Library Association provides—projects such as Voices and Visions or Poets in Person. ALA's application process is relatively easy and the training provided for these demonstration projects is important. (a sample ALA application form/project description is shown in Appendix D.) It is a great way to begin. Statewide and system approaches are also good. For example, NEH funds the Peninsula Library System in California and the Southern Connecticut Library System and the programs are delivered to small town libraries. If small libraries want to start humanities programs it is probably better to work with the state humanities council. They are closer, and can provide more "hand holding" to help people get started. Some state councils have more staff than we do.

What you really need to get started is a good idea. You know what your library can do, and you get help to do it. Your program doesn't have to be a "Let's Talk About It" type of reading and discussion program. New Rochelle (New York) came up with a lecture series on Tom Paine because he was born there. They recruited scholars. They needed more money than the state council could provide, so they came to NEH.

Q: *When should a library apply to NEH and when to the state humanities council?*

A: There isn't any one simple answer to that question. It is usually answered in terms of dollars—national grants being larger than state grants—but that isn't necessarily always true. State councils require a 50 percent cost share, but it can be in-kind. NEH does not have this requirement. We just need to know that the institution is committed to the project.

You get a closer relationship and probably more direct assistance at the state level. I will provide help to librarians developing or implementing projects, but I have only so much time. I have never seen a state council turn down a project if someone has sat with them in their living room. The proposal may not be funded the first time around, but it will be eventually. It's important to remember, though, that state councils are *councils*, and they tend to have councilors who are more involved than our councilors are at the national level. The staff can advise, but the councilors make the final decisions. (The proposal in Appendix E from the Merced (California) County Library is an example of a mini-grant funded by the California Council for the Humanities.)

Q: *What kind of assistance can librarians receive from the state council?*

A: Every kind of assistance! If you have a decent idea, the state council staff will help you develop it. They'll help you find the people to consult on your idea. They will refer to you to scholars. They will get involved. All you need to get started is an idea.

Q: *What is the best way to get acquainted?*

A: Make a phone call. Say, "Hi, here's my idea. Our mission is to develop educational programs and here's one I think you ought to fund." We love those phone calls. If I don't think NEH can fund the idea, I'll recommend a funding source. I feel like I'm being called with a reference question, and you can be sure I'm ready to help and will find an answer. Part of getting acquainted involves discovering the funding agenda of the agency. You have to be able to give and take a bit. We may like your idea but ask you to make some changes.

Q: *What kind of library projects does NEH fund?*

A: NEH funds educational programs in the humanities. Librarians are most familiar with reading and discussion programs in the "Let's Talk About It" tradition, but we also fund lecture series, chautauquas, exhibitions, and we want to fund seminars in the humanities. There are new guidelines for library programs, and I'll gladly send a copy to anyone who is interested.

Q: *The conventional wisdom is that NEH grants are a great deal of work. Do you think this is true? How can you help?*

A: They are work, but not *too* much work. Developing a proposal involves thinking through the whole project, and that's not so terrible if someone is holding your hand. Very few projects are funded that we have not helped develop. We are here to help. Even when proposals come in "over the transom" we send them through the regular review process, so they receive feedback from staff and the review panel. Proposals turned down that are re-submitted have about a 90 percent success rate.

Q: *What kind of proposals are you looking for?*

A: Good ones! I want proposals that define libraries as educational institutions—encouraging people to read good literature and history—that show libraries as part of the learning society.

Q: *What do you mean by quality proposals?*

A: We look for quality in the content—the humanities scholarship—and we want to be convinced that the library is capable of carrying out the project. We look for a good idea that will provide educational services to a target group. It should also help the library carry out its own mission. A quality proposal has both good content and a manageable process. It has achievable goals and a good plan of work.

Q: *What are the odds of getting funded by NEH?*

A: NEH library programs in Washington fund about one in three proposals submitted. As I mentioned, 90 percent of re-submissions are funded, especially when people use the evaluation comments to strengthen their proposal. State councils fund about 50 percent of proposals and offer lots of guidance for re-submission.

Q: *What are the most common errors that cause proposals to be rejected?*

A: In our case, bad scholarship. We have scholars on the panels that review proposals. They look for solid scholarly content. Other proposals are rejected because they don't have a well thought out plan—a problem that is easier for librarians to solve!

To ensure that the content ideas are convincing, it is best to involve a scholar who understands the disciplines and methodologies of the humanities in preparing the proposal. Use a team approach for the project and demonstrate it in your proposal. Scholars can't always plan programs, and librarians may not be able to define thematic content, but the partnership works.

Q: *Do you think it is important for applicants to be aware of the proposal review process at NEH?*

A: It doesn't hurt! The more you want success in any kind of proposal process, the more you want to know about the funder, their agenda, and how they work. At NEH we have peer review panels with scholars looking at scholarly content and librarians reviewing program design. You don't need to know who the people are, but it is good to know the process. After the review panels, NEH proposals go to the National Council on the Humanities, 26 men and women appointed by the President and confirmed by the Senate. The whole process is described in the guidelines. The final authority rests with the chairman. Almost all proposals given high marks by the panel are funded.

You need to know that the goals of your proposal and the funding agency are a good match. You wouldn't go to NEH to launch a football team, build a rocket, or study the environment. But if you want to study the environment through the literature or look at the history and social meaning of sports, we'd like to talk with you. You need to ask yourself, "Why do they want to give money to me? Do I want to do what they want to fund? Do librarians really want to do educational programs? Is it a part of our library's mission?"

Q: *What is your general view of librarians and the whole grant-seeking process—any general advice?*

A: I think librarians are afraid. I think they are fearful of the process. Also, they don't think they should have to raise money to do what they want to do. Between the fear and the arrogance, seeking funds becomes a big deal rather than the routine pattern of operating that it is for other people or organizations. I sense librarians saying to themselves, "Libraries are so good that I shouldn't have to ask for support." Nonsense! Once they get started, librarians are exceptionally good at program development and proposal writing, and can be very successful.

Museum people have been down here a long time, have gotten past that kind of blockage, and can get money all over the place. There are 16,000 fewer museums than libraries in this country (if you count public and academic libraries), but the NEH museum program gets four times the number of proposals as the library program. Hence they get more money. We need more good library proposals.

Please tell people to write for the guidelines for programs in libraries and archives and for challenge grants. And tell them to call me for help. Here's my address and phone number:

Thomas Phelps
Senior Program Officer
Division of Public Programs
National Endowment for the Humanities
1100 Pennsylvania Avenue, N.W.
Washington, DC 20506
202-606-8271

5 FOUNDATION FUNDING

There are over 27,000 nonprofit organizations in the United States designated as "private foundations" or "community foundations" that award grants to other nonprofit organizations to promote the public good. Private and community foundations awarded over $123 million in grants to support a wide range of programs in public, university, school, and special libraries in 1990. Whether you are looking for funds to operate a new program, build or renovate library space, purchase new materials or equipment, or host a conference or seminar, foundations can be an important funding source for your library. These foundations fall into four basic categories.

Independent Foundations: Funds are usually derived from a single source, such as an individual or a family. Some of these foundations are known as "family foundations" and members of the original donor's family serve on the foundation board or staff and provide strong direction for the foundation's giving. Others, like The Ford Foundation or The Rockefeller Foundation, are no longer directed by family members and have relatively broad discretion in carrying out the grant-making mission of the original donor. These foundations may focus their giving in a few specified subject areas or they may award grants for a wide variety of programs. About 70 percent limit their giving to a specific local area, usually the state or community in which they are located.

Company-sponsored Foundations: Legally independent organizations funded by a corporation. These foundations usually have close ties to the corporation providing the funds and their giving tends to be in fields related to the interests of the corporation or in regions where the corporation operates.

Operating Foundations: Generally these foundations manage or operate their own research or service programs, such as a museum or a performance space, and seldom make grants to other organizations.

Community Foundations: Funds are derived from many individuals and corporations within their local community and grants are awarded to organizations or programs that specifically benefit that community. Most of these foundations operate under slightly different tax laws than private foundations, but their grant-making programs are very similar. Many community foundations are very involved with local nonprofit organizations, providing management assistance and advice on fundraising in addition to their grant-making programs.

Before you can apply for a foundation grant, you need to find out which foundations are willing to support organizations in your state or community for the type of program you are offering; the size and type of grants those foundations are willing to make; and how to apply for grant support. While they share many common characteristics, every foundation is unique with its own specific giving interests and restrictions and its own application procedures and deadlines. Your success in getting a grant will often depend on how much you know about the funder.

Your search should begin at one of the 176 cooperating libraries of The Foundation Center, a national service organization supported by the foundation community to provide information and assistance to grant seekers. In addition to the four major library centers staffed and maintained by The Foundation Center in New York, Washington, D.C., Cleveland, and San Francisco, the Center maintains a nationwide network of library collections to provide free, convenient access to their own directories, indexes, and other publications on foundations and grants, as well as publications produced by foundation and corporate grant-makers and important reference sources issued by other publishers. Many of these libraries have trained staff and offer free orientation programs to help you get started with your research. For information about the resources and services nearest you, call 1-800-424-9836 (in New York State, call 212-620-4230).

There are entire books devoted to explaining how to research and get foundation grants, some of which are listed in the bibliography, but don't let yourself get discouraged by long or complicated explanations. The following outline may help to put the process into perspective.

Begin Close to Home: Foundations that have stated or demonstrated an interest in supporting programs in your state or community are usually your best place to start. Find out if there is a *current* directory of foundations located in your state or region (out-of-date information can often mislead). If not, most directories of foundations and/or foundation grants include a geographic index to guide you to foundations that are located in or have awarded grants to organizations in your area.

Make Sure Your Interests are Compatible: Look for foundations that have stated, or demonstrated through their grants, an interest in libraries or the type of program you are proposing. Start with the directories of grants for libraries, such as The Foundation Center's publication *National Guide to Funding for Libraries and Information Services*, a listing of major foundations and their recent grants to libraries. But don't limit yourself to foundations that have already supported libraries. A foundation that is interested in improving health services might be willing to support a library program to disseminate information about health care to the broader community. A foundation interested in children or education might fund a new library reading program, a homework help service, or an outreach service to help parents become stronger partners in their children's education. Let your creative energies go to work as you consult the subject indexes of foundation directories or examine the giving interests or grants lists of foundations in your area.

Find Out All You Can: Get as much information about each likely foundation from the directories and indexes of grants available in your local library or grants office. The Foundation checklist in Worksheet 5-1 shows the type of information you should gather. Then find out what the foundation says about itself in its annual report, application guidelines, newsletters or other publications. If your library doesn't have these materials, write or call the foundation directly to ask for their most recent annual report or grant application information. You can also check the foundation's tax return, known as IRS Form 990-PF, a public document that is available in most Foundation Center libraries, to get a listing of recent grants, giving interests, and other key information.

Enlist Some Allies: First assemble basic information about a few foundations that might be interested in funding your program—and that don't have restrictions that would prevent their supporting your library. Then find out if any of your board, staff, volunteers, or current contributors know any staff or board members at the foundation. A personal connection can be valuable for getting advice about how to submit your application or finding the right person to tell about the program you are proposing. Talk to project directors at other organizations who have received grants from your target foundation. They can often help you get your foot in the door so you can explain your idea to a program officer or other staff member of the foundation. It always helps to get as much informed guidance as possible to develop the type of proposal or funding request that will get the foundation's interest and attention.

WORKSHEET 5-1

FOUNDATION RESEARCH CHECKLIST

FOUNDATION NAME:
ADDRESS:

TELEPHONE:
GRANT APPLICATION ADDRESS (IF DIFFERENT)

CONTACT PERSON:
MEMBERS OF BOARD OF DIRECTORS:

KEY STAFF MEMBERS:

TOTAL NUMBER OF GRANTS AND DOLLARS AWARDED:
AVERAGE SIZE OR RANGE OF GRANTS:
APPLICATION GUIDELINES/DEADLINES:

STATES/CITIES WHERE IT MAKES GRANTS:

TYPES OF ORGANIZATIONS IT FUNDS:

TYPES OF PROGRAMS IT FUNDS:

RESTRICTIONS ON GIVING (IF ANY):

GRANTS AWARDED TO LIBRARIES OR FOR PROGRAMS SIMILAR TO
OURS:

So you see it's not that complicated. Yes, it takes time, but the rewards for your library can be great. Even if a foundation is unable to provide a grant, your contacts may be able to help you get support from other funders. So use the following list of resources and get going!

RESOURCES

The Foundation Directory. The oldest and best-known of all foundation directories is published by The Foundation Center. It provides financial and application information as well as general descriptions of the nation's 7,500 largest foundations (those awarding at least $100,000 in grants annually or with assets of $1 million or more). It includes indexes by geographic location and subject interests. It's available in all Foundation Center libraries and cooperating collections or it can be purchased for $150 plus $4.50 shipping and handling ($175 for hardcover) from The Foundation Center, 79 Fifth Avenue, New York, N.Y. 10003-3050.

The Foundation Directory, Part Two. A recent addition from The Foundation Center, this guide provides information on over 4,200 mid-sized foundations (those with annual giving between $25,000 and $100,000). Descriptions drawn from foundation tax returns are supplemented by listings of recent grants and other information provided by the foundations. It, too, can be used in Foundation Center libraries or purchased for $150 plus $4.50 shipping and handling from The Foundation Center.

The Foundation Grants Index. This Foundation Center publication lists over 55,000 grants of $10,000 or more awarded by over 750 of the nation's largest foundations with indexes by the name and geographic location of organizations receiving grants, the subject focus of the grant, and the type of support awarded (scholarships, building funds, endowments, exhibitions, etc.) Like other Foundation Center publications, it can be used in their libraries or purchased for $125 plus $4.50 shipping and handling.

National Guide to Funding for Libraries and Information Services. Also from The Foundation Center, this guide provides a quick reference to the over 400 foundations and corporate giving programs listed in *The Foundation Directory* and/or *The Foundation Grants Index* that have awarded grants to libraries or information services in other organizations. The grant listings can be an excellent source of ideas about the types of library programs that have been supported by foundations.

The Directory of Corporate and Foundation Givers. This guide provides descriptive profiles of 8,000 foundations and corporate-giving programs with nine indexes and ten short essays on trends in foundation and corporate giving. It's also available in many libraries or you can purchase it for $195 from the Fund Raising Institute Division, The Taft Group, 12300

Twinbrook Parkway, Suite 450, Rockville, MD 20852-9830 (or call 800-877-8238).

State Directories

State directories of foundation and corporate grant-makers are available from a wide variety of publishers. To find out whether there is a directory of foundations specifically for your state or region, contact your local Foundation Center cooperating collection. Some of the oldest and best known state directories include:

Connecticut Foundation Directory, 1990-1991. $50 plus $4 shipping. D.A.T.A., 70 Audubon Street, New Haven, CT 06510. (203-772-1345)

Directory of Missouri Foundations. $35. Metropolitan Association for Philanthropy, 5585 Pershing, Suite 150, St. Louis, MO 63112. (314-361-3900)

Directory of Texas Foundations. $119 plus $2 shipping. Funding Information Center, 507 Brooklyn, San Antonio, TX 78215. (512-227-4333)

The Michigan Foundation Directory. $25. Michigan League for Human Services, 300 North Washington Square, Suite 401, Lansing, MI 48933.

New York State Foundations, Second Edition. $150 plus $4.50 shipping and handling. The Foundation Center, 79 Fifth Avenue, New York, NY 10003-3050. (800-424-9836)

INTERVIEW

RUTH CAINE, BELL ATLANTIC

Over breakfast in Washington, D.C. we talked with Ruth Caine, who was then Director of the Bell Atlantic Charitable Foundation. It is a relatively new corporate foundation, established in 1987. In 1989 they made 73 grants ranging from $1,000 to $300,000 plus $631,734 for employee matching grants. They have provided major grant support to the American Library Association for the Bell Atlantic/ALA Family Literacy Project. Ruth Caine was a full partner in developing the Family Literacy Project and it was a joy to work with her. Here she talks about the foundation and how grant making looks from the funder's perspective:

Q: *What kind of grants does your foundation make?*

A: We focus on literacy programming and science and technology education. We believe it is important to decide on a specific focus and stick with it. We fund special projects and very seldom give an organization ongoing support.

Q: *Do you have an application procedure?*

A: Early-on we developed an application form, but we quickly found it to be unusable. Now, we encourage people to send an overview before submitting a proposal. We want to know what the proposed project is for, who it will serve, and why it is needed. It is also helpful for us to know if other funding is available. We frequently receive letters that don't answer any of these questions, so we turn them down.

Q: *How many inquiries do you receive and how many projects do you fund?*

A: Last year we received 1,200 requests and gave 101 grants. More than 300 of those requests were invitations to purchase tables at fund raisers—we hardly ever do that. You get the feeling people send form letters to every foundation. I have received as many as 100 inquiries in one day. That's a lot when you consider that grant activity is only 30 to 40 percent of my job. You've got to convince us, because we don't have time to make your case.

Q: *Does your board review all proposals that are funded?*

A: Only proposals over $50,000 have to go to our board—and then only proposals that we are recommending for funding. We never ask them to review more than three to eight projects. But you can be sure the board members carefully evaluate these major projects and ask serious questions. We always have a personal relationship with the organization before their proposal goes to our board. At times we have brought in people from the applicant organization to make presentations to the board.

Rather than giving a total proposal to the board we prepare a capsule version describing the project, the budget, background on the organization, a communications plan, and our recommendation.

Q: *Do you visit agencies that request grants?*

A: We frequently visit agencies that we might be considering for major grants, especially if we need to get a sense of how effectively they are operated. I once visited an organization in New York that was total chaos.

Q: *What makes you interested in an organization?*

A: Something about their overall purpose will make us interested, especially if they can help us carry out projects in our areas of special focus. As a relationship develops, the project we fund may turn out to be quite different from what they originally proposed.

Occasionally we issue an RFP if we are trying to find organizations to do specific projects. Organizations don't always come to us. We often make the first approach.

Q: *Please talk more about routine rejections.*

A: A lot of the inquiries we receive are not in our areas of interest. It is clear that many people don't do their homework. We don't even respond to "broadcast" letters. If it is a specially written letter we will answer it. We receive many unsolicited proposals. We look at the cover letter, and if it is interesting, give it to a staff person to do an analysis.

Q: *Does it bother you if people make follow-up calls?*

A: Not really. We're short staffed—most corporate foundations are short staffed. The call may inspire us to find the letter in the stacks of mail. Some people write letters that say they will follow up with a call on a specific day. I put these in a convenient place so I'll be ready for the call. If they don't call, I certainly notice it!

Q: *What are the most common mistakes?*

A: People think they know their project is consistent with our aims—and they are wrong. In full proposals the main idea is too often tucked away on page seven. And there is often too much background about the organization. Proposals don't have to be long. They do have to be clear and straightforward, e.g., this is what we're looking for—this is why.

We like to provide value back to the jurisdictions we serve. We are looking for quality projects. We are new at grant making, but I've already learned that there is a lot of difference in style and philosophy in how foundations operate. Yet I'm sure we all want to invest our funds wisely in organizations of quality and integrity.

Following are the applicant review criteria from the policy and procedure manual of the Bell Atlantic Charitable Foundation:

APPLICANT REVIEW CRITERIA

Each organization applying for support from the Bell Atlantic Foundation will be evaluated on its own merit and in terms of its relevance to the Foundation's program priorities. Consideration will be given to the organization's financial and administrative condition, as well as to the proposed program or project for which support is requested.

Financial and Administrative Criteria

1. Financial stability, as evidenced by:
   - Financial statements for prior years, preferably prepared by an outside auditor and accompanied by a sound auditor's report;
   - Assets equal to or exceeding debt; and
   - Other stable sources of income and preferably an operating reserve fund that is properly invested.
2. Financial planning and management capacity, as indicated by:
   - Close adherence to prior years' projected budgets;
   - Absence of operating deficits; and

- Availability of staff or contracted services to ensure sound accounting for income and expenses.
3. Appropriate governance and oversight, as indicated by:
   - Expertise represented on Board of Directors; and
   - Frequency and nature of board meetings;
4. Overall administration and project management capacity, as indicated by:
   - Qualifications and experience of key personnel;
   - Level of involvement of top management in proposed project; and
   - Qualifications of staff assigned to proposed project.

Program Criteria

- Clearly documented need;
- Realistic, attainable goals and objectives for the program;
- Work plan that clearly addresses the program objectives;
- Services or activities that complement rather than duplicate those offered by other organizations;
- Adequate budget for carrying out programs;
- Plan for evaluating results of program; and
- Plan for continuing project after the Foundation's support concludes.

6 CORPORATE FUNDING

One of our vice presidents serves on the library foundation board. He likes it. He's in love with the library. After all, what's not to love about the library?

Roberta Weinstein
Pubic Affairs Manager,
American Express

Corporate giving offers great potential for libraries, but has the fewest rules or guidelines. It can vary from corporate foundation grants to launch a project or build a building, to publicity and small contributions from cause-related marketing campaigns. The most important thing to remember about corporate giving is—keep the self interest of the funder in mind. Think partnership. A proposal to a corporation should emphasize how the project will help them achieve company goals. Don't be arrogant. There is nothing wrong with a company exercising good business judgment. Just be clear on your own goals, and choose your partners carefully. Be prepared to provide consistent, visible credit for corporate gifts. Follow-up and follow through.

SOME EXAMPLES

The Mott's Library Reading Program is a recent example of a cause-related marketing opportunity offered to libraries in the fall of 1992 with the cooperation of Friends of Libraries U.S.A. Between September and November 1992, Mott's urged library friends to collect proofs-of-purchase from their products, which the library could redeem for books. Information about the project sent to participating libraries is shown in Figure 6-1, to give you an idea of how these programs typically work. In most cases, national cause-related marketing opportunities are promoted to librarians by direct mail. Many similar programs are developed locally. The possibilities are endless.

The Cargill/ALA Family Literacy Project is another kind of corporate/library project. Cargill Incorporated is a giant agricultural company with more than 53,000 employees at 800 locations in 55 countries. A corporate contribution to ALA helped produce materials about family literacy that were mailed to librarians and Cargill managers in the communities where Cargill is present. Cargill seeks employee involvement in local programs. In the first months of the project more than 138 local programs have been

FIGURE 6-1   Mott's Free Books Program Materials

MOTT'S U.S.A.

6 HIGH RIDGE PARK
POST OFFICE BOX 3800
STAMFORD, CONNECTICUT 06905-0800

PHONE (203) 968-7500
TELEX 965904
FAX (203) 968-7653

Dear Library Program Participant:

Mott's® USA is proud to announce that the response to our 1992 Library Program has been tremendous (approximately 3,000 participating libraries nationwide) and we're glad that you're a part of it. We're also pleased to inform you that current plans are for Mott's to fulfill your free book orders with Baker & Taylor, the nation's leading book wholesaler. All you do is collect Mott's proofs-of-purchase (UPC codes) and send them to us at the conclusion of the program -- we'll organize the rest.

Now, however, it's time to get to the business of helping you earn as many free books and educational materials as possible. Enclosed is a support kit containing all the promotional materials your library needs to maximize its proof collection (remember, the more Mott's proofs you collect, the more free books your library receives). We've also provided simple recommendations on how to involve your community by using local publicity.

As an added bonus from Mott's, your library has been automatically entered to win one of ten $1,000 grants which will be awarded by a random drawing in December, 1992.

Please review the attached pages for a more complete description of the Library Program and for recommendations on how to best use the components of this kit. Should any questions arise, please feel free to call us toll free at 1-800-845-2405.

Once again, thanks for your participation. All of us at Mott's wish you great success!

Sincerely,

Carl Harrington
Vice President, Mott's Marketing

A MEMBER OF THE CADBURY SCHWEPPES PLC GROUP

FIGURE 6-1   Mott's Free Books Program Materials, Cont.

"Friends of Libraries U.S.A. is delighted to participate in the Mott's® Library Reading Program. It provides great benefits and community awareness for libraries. Mott's® makes a great partner."
—Sandy Dolnick, Executive Director, FOLUSA

BUSINESS REPLY MAIL
FIRST-CLASS MAIL PERMIT NO. 208 RIVERTON, NJ

POSTAGE WILL BE PAID BY ADDRESSEE

MOTT's® Library Reading Program
P.O. Box 721
Riverton, NJ 08077-9923

PO Box 721
Riverton, NJ 08077-0721

09231-000 02/93 03
PEGGY BARBER
AMRICAN LIBRARY ASSN
50 E. HURON ST
CHICAGO, IL
60611

MOTT'S. INTRODUCES A NOVEL IDEA:

FREE
BOOKS FOR YOUR LIBRARY!
WITH PROOFS-OF-PURCHASE

INTRODUCING AN EXCITING LIBRARY PROGRAM JUST FOR YOU.

MOTT'S. USA, a longtime sponsor of reading and educational programs, is proud to announce the Mott's® Library Reading Program, a unique opportunity for Americans to support their local library.

Up to $500,000 worth of books and other library materials can be earned among participating libraries nationwide!

At Mott's®, we recognize the value of your efforts on behalf of the library in your community. In cooperation with Friends of Libraries U.S.A., we've designed a special program to support you: The Mott's® Library Reading Program. By participating in this exciting new Program, you can help your library become eligible to receive free books and other library materials. And it's easy!

With the help of library users, your library simply needs to collect proofs-of-purchase from any of the following Mott's® products: Mott's® Apple Juice, Juice Boxes, Apple Sauce and Single Serve Apple Sauce Fruit Snacks. **Each Mott's® proof will be worth 25¢ towards the retail value of library books/materials.** The more proofs collected, the more books/materials your library receives!

WIN AN EXTRA BONUS!

As a bonus for participating in the Mott's® Library Reading Program, your library will automatically become eligible to win one of ten $1,000 grants, to be awarded at random at the conclusion of the Program.

HOW DOES THE PROGRAM WORK?

After receiving your commitment to participate, Mott's® will send your library a special FREE kit containing everything you need to implement the 12-week program, scheduled to run from September through November, 1992. Included in this kit will be:

- a letter describing the Program in detail
- a generous supply of *Parent Pages*, a newsletter which encourages reading, storytelling and library usage, for distribution in your library
- a poster announcing a vacation sweepstakes for library users
- a press release your library can adapt and localize
- a list of ideas for individualizing the Program and promoting reading in your library
- reproducible artwork for use in your library fliers and mailings
- an attractive collection box for proofs-of-purchase
- a proof-of-purchase tally form and return envelope

At the conclusion of the Program, you simply count the proofs, fill out the tally form and send the envelope with proofs to Mott's®. Your library will then be given a credit certificate redeemable through a national book wholesaler. It's just that simple! Get your Friends group involved NOW!

INTERESTED? LET US HEAR FROM YOU.

If you and your library are interested in participating in the Mott's® Library Reading Program, please fill out the following form and mail it (postage free) back to Mott's® by **May 22, 1992**. We'll send you the complete program kit in August!

Make your plans now! If you have any questions before returning this Business Reply Card, please call toll free **800-845-2405.**

☐ **YES**, we would like to participate in the Mott's® 1992 Library Reading Program.

Library Name:

Library Address:

City:

State: Zip:

Contact Person:

Phone Number (Optional):

Address Where Kit Should Be Sent:

Attention:

Your Comments or Suggestions:

If you do not intend to participate in this program but would like your library to become eligible for a $1,000 grant, please mail a self-addressed, stamped envelope by May 22, 1992 to: Mott's® Library Reading Program, P.O. Box 721, Riverton, NJ 08077-0721 to receive an official entry form.

© 1992 Cadbury Beverages Inc.   AJ-91

FIGURE 6-1   Mott's Free Books Program Materials, Cont.

MOTT'S 1992 LIBRARY READING PROGRAM

OVERVIEW

- Mott's® USA -- in cooperation with Friends of Libraries, U.S.A. -- will provide up to $500,000 to America's public libraries for the purchase of books and educational materials.

- The Mott's Library Program is designed to be fun and easy to implement. Your library simply collects Mott's proofs-of-purchase from now until November 30, 1992.

- Each Mott's proof is worth 25¢ toward the retail value of books and materials*.

- In mid-November, we'll send you a package containing instructions for redeeming your proofs, a tally sheet for reporting your collection totals, and a postage-paid envelope for submitting your proofs to Mott's.

- After we receive your proofs, Mott's will send you a credit voucher and ordering procedures from our chosen book supplier.

KIT CONTENTS/DESCRIPTION

- PROOF COLLECTION BOX (requires minimal assembly - 1 included)

  Colorfully designed to call attention to the program and remind library users to save proofs and bring them in. Display the box where it's clearly visible and easily accessible for depositing proofs. Empty the collection box as needed. Proofs are valuable (worth 25¢ each) and should be kept in a safe place until the program concludes on November 30, 1992.

- "HELP YOUR LIBRARY" POSTER (1 included)

  Display the poster in a prominent, high traffic area in your library to create awareness for the program and stimulate library users to begin saving Mott's proofs.

- "PARENT PAGES" NEWSLETTERS (300 included)

  This popular Mott's family newsletter features entertaining and educational information and encourages families to share the joy of reading. This edition has been specially printed to explain how to help your library receive free books. Distribute newsletters during library activities or display as a free take-one.

FIGURE 6-1   Mott's Free Books Program Materials, Cont.

- <u>BOOKMARKS (300 included)</u>

  Use as gifts or prizes for library users. This attractive bookmark extends the positive message that "reading is a good thing!"

- <u>"HELP OUR LIBRARY" STAFF BUTTONS (5 included)</u>

  Buttons encourage people to ask questions about the program and participate. Distribute them to your staff.

- <u>PRESS RELEASE (1 included)</u>

  This official Mott's Press Release highlights the program and raises awareness concerning the current fiscal struggle faced by America's libraries. Make copies and submit them to local newspapers and radio stations to spread the word. Be sure to insert your library's name (and story) into the release so that readers and listeners know how they can help.

- <u>BLACK & WHITE FLYER (1 included)</u>

  This reproducible bulletin can be used as a mailing piece, memo or poster. Remember to insert your library's name in the space provided.

- <u>COMMUNITY INVOLVEMENT IDEA SHEET (1 included)</u>

  We've also provided a number of ideas to help your library gain the large-scale support of area merchants, schools, local clubs and other community groups. Please use these as a starting point to generate excitement and build community involvement.

*   Should the program's total national budget cap of $500,000 be reached (which we do not anticipate occurring) Mott's will reduce its per proof contribution to participating libraries on a proportional basis.

launched, and Cargill divisions have contributed more than $200,000 to these local efforts.

A newsletter from the Queens Borough (New York) Public Library dated spring 1992 describes a local corporate marketing project that benefitted the library. Brooklyn Union Gas donated $5,950 to the library on behalf of the 238 Queens homeowners who switched from oil to gas heat during September, October, and November 1991. For each conversion $25 was donated to the library system in the homeowner's borough. "This donation program not only provided Queens Library with desperately needed money, it also raised awareness among Queens residents of the work the Library does," commented library director Constance B. Cooke. "The very welcome donation, and others provided by Brooklyn Union Gas, has helped keep programs alive that, sadly, might otherwise have been lost due to funding cuts."

In another corporate giving program the Bank of America made contributions to the California State Library Foundation when customers purchased a new check product series. The contributions, totaling $64,000, then became grants to California public libraries to help develop literacy programs. (See Figure 6-2.)

HOW TO START

How are corporate partnerships developed? A conference on Library Foundations and Development Efforts sponsored in the spring of 1992 by the Council for Florida Libraries, Inc., the Broward County Library, and the Broward Public Library Foundation brought in their corporate friends to present real live information about how it happens. The speakers included the media—*Sun Sentinel* Newspaper; a *Fortune 500* company—American Express; and a major corporate citizen—Barnett Bank of Broward County.

The library foundation carefully picked its partners and went after them. They developed real projects from within the library, that offered visibility and clear benefits to their business partners. The needs of the library were shaped into salable packages by the library foundation staff. They have worked so well with their initial corporate partners that others needed to get on the library's band wagon.

The *Sun Sentinel's* promotion manager, Mary Reidel, said "I'm not selling newspapers anymore, I'm working for the library." She made it clear that the partnership with the library is based on enlightened self interest and good personal relationships. Working with the library has enhanced the image of the newspaper and enabled them to set themselves apart from the competition. There

FIGURE 6-2   Bank of America Literary Project

CALIFORNIA
STATE
LIBRARY
FOUNDATION

PRESERVING,

PROTECTING

AND PROMOTING

CALIFORNIA'S

RICH CULTURAL

HERITAGE

...... FOR IMMEDIATE RELEASE

INNOVATIVE ADULT LITERACY INSTRUCTION SUPPORTED THROUGH PUBLIC/PRIVATE PARTNERSHIP AWARDS

SACRAMENTO, August 21, 1992 -- The California State Library Foundation and the Bank of America today announced awards totaling nearly $64,000 which will help develop innovative approaches to adult literacy instruction in California.

Gary E. Strong, State Librarian of California, said, "We are very pleased and excited by the results of a marketing initiative created by Bank of America in collaboration with libraries of the California Literacy Campaign. These funds will help fuel innovations in adult literacy instruction which will benefit all Californians."

The awards were made possible from dollars generated during the past two years by customer purchases of a new check product series created by the Bank of America in the fall of 1989. A portion of each new product purchased was contributed to the Literacy Fund of the California State Library Foundation.

-more-

(916) 654-0174

P.O. Box 942837

SACRAMENTO, CA

94237-0001

FIGURE 6-2   Bank of America Literary Project, Cont.

Bank of America Vice Chairman Thomas E. Peterson, head of the Consumer Banking Group, said, "We applaud the California State Library for joining us to make this partnership possible, and we warmly congratulate each of the award winners for the creative new programs they have designed that address the adult literacy needs in their communities."

A rigorous proposal review process resulted in four awards being made at this time:

• The South San Francisco Public Library's Multi-sensory Tutor Training Workshop program was awarded a $7,200 grant to extend training for adult educators and tutors across California.

• The Santa Clara County Library received $11,280 to help fund computer-aided literacy instruction for adults in Santa Clara County correctional facilities and recovery houses.

• A $25,000 grant to the Escondido Public Library will fund special education intervention with developmentally disabled adults.

• A grant totaling $20,229 will be used to fund a writing skills program being developed by the National City and Chula Vista public libraries.

###

Contact:
Gary E. Strong (916) 654-0174, State Librarian of California
Harvey Radin (415) 622-6320, Bank of America
Paul Kiley (916) 324-7358, California State Library

FIGURE 6-2   Bank of America Literary Project, Cont.

CALIFORNIA STATE LIBRARY FOUNDATION

Literacy Projects Awarded Funds

The California State Library Foundation Board of Directors awarded funds in the amount of $63,709.50 to four projects from its California Literacy Fund established with the Bank of America. The projects are:

Reading Program of Santa Clara County Library for $11,280.50
    "Adult Learners in Recovery Houses"
    Total Project Budget is $25,246.00. It is a one-year project.
Description: The Reading Program, is a library-based literacy program providing one-on-one tutoring to English speaking adults 16 years and older in the community, county correctional facilities, and Santa Clara County Recovery Houses. Funds will be used to provide learners in one of the recovery houses with a computer-aided literacy instruction as a supplement to their one-on-one tutoring. The computer-aided instruction enhances on-site tutoring and enables the learners to work independently at the work stations. In addition to improved literacy skills, learners are introduced to basic computer skills in a friendly environment.

South San Francisco Public Library for $7,200.00
    "Regional Training Workshops"
    Total Project Budget is $11,400. It is a one-year project.
Description: The purpose is to share a successful tutor training model and set of tutor support materials which have been developed to teach tutors and learners how to create multisensory lessons which involve the learner's intelligences and learning styles. Six workshops will be conducted throughout California to offer one-day training for staff, tutors, and learners about using the materials that can then be used independently in lessons with learners.

National City Public Library for $20,229
    "Adult Learners With Low Writing Skills"
    Total Project Budget is $24,379. It is a one-year project.
Description: National City Public Library and Chula Vista Public Library will develop model, small-group writing classes designed to address the lack of personal and practical writing skills in adult learners in library literacy programs. The classes will be taught by an experienced mentor instructor, and will be based on current educational research in writing as a precess, and using a "Whole Language" framework. The second component will videotape the teaching process and incorporate it into the tutor training curriculum. Tutors will learn the methodology through didactic presentations and hands-on practice under the supervision of the mentor instructor.

Escondido Public Library for $25,000
    "Adults with Developmental Disabilities"
    Total Project Budget is $30,224. It is a nine month project.
Description: The San Diego Council on Literacy Committee to Serve Adults with Developmental Disabilities will train life skills workers to provide reading instruction to some of their clients who are developmentally disabled. Caseworkers will tutor two to four clients on their caseloads on their home visits. READ/2000 staff will pre and post-test to measure reading progress. Each worker will be interviewed to determine what methods of reading instruction were most effective after nine months of tutoring. With the growing number of developmentally disabled adults entering library literacy programs, the experience from this project will provide valuable information which will be disseminated.

is a strong common interest in literacy. The library represents broad community interest and support—including multicultural support—also important to the newspaper.

It all started over lunch. It was clear that all the activities were planned together. One of their projects was *Year of the Young Reader* with a series of events every month including a spring *Children's Reading Festival*. Many corporate partners worked on a myriad of special events. The *Reading Festival* has continued for four years and the audience for concerts, readings and other events has quadrupled. A local drug store chain has also gotten involved and provides a *Great Book Giveaway*, providing great visibility for their stores and free books for kids.

Reidel mentioned that the library partnership offers her company quantifiable results in visibility and increased sales. She made it clear that: "It is a business deal. It is not corporate philanthropy." She also made it clear that chemistry is very important. She and the library foundation director like each other, respect each other, and have had a great time working together.

All of the corporate partners on the Broward County program spoke of the library and library foundation staff with great affection, respect, and solid understanding. They described the library as a strong institution with excellent visibility and outreach throughout the county. The library also offers opportunities for employees of their business partner to become involved. They described rewarding experiences and mutually beneficial projects. They explained why the library was a sound marketing choice. One of the speakers said, "The personal approach is worth a thousand letters." It all started over lunch. (Don't forget to pick up the tab for lunch!)

For more information on the amazing Broward County Library Foundation experience, contact Kay Harvey, Executive Director, Broward County Library Foundation, Inc., 100 South Andrews Ave. Fort Lauderdale, FL 33301. 305-357-7469.

7 DEVELOPING YOUR PROPOSAL

Stop! *Do not write a proposal before a funder has requested it*. It *is* who you know that counts. The proposals most likely to be funded are those developed *with* a funder.

While contemplating the proposal writing process, we realized that we have never had one funded that was submitted cold. There has always been an initial stage of work with a program officer to discuss and develop the project idea. In addition to helping you fine-tune the idea, a program officer will let you know about the proposal review process and any specific guidelines or forms.

PROSPECTING LETTER

When you have developed a good idea and have researched potential funders, see if you can find someone who knows someone to make an introduction. If there is no potential for personal contact, the best approach is a letter—one page if possible. Your succinct prospecting letter should state the problem, how you plan to solve it, explain why your library is uniquely suited to implement the grant project, and ask if the foundation or corporation would like to receive a proposal. A sample prospecting letter and the response to it are shown in Figure 7-1.

Writing a prospecting letter is much like explaining your great idea to a total stranger. Put the emphasis on the problem and how you plan to solve it rather than on you or your organization. Be brief and straightforward. The potential funder doesn't need to know that the project is within your library's mission or strategic long range plan—that can come later. Keep your attention on the funder's point of view as you write the letter. Remember, your greatest challenge is to get their attention. Statistics may help describe the problem, but a meaningful human interest story might have more impact. Don't be shy. Go for drama.

Should the prospecting letter indicate how much money you are looking for? Good question! If you have developed a general idea of the budget requirements, you might as well say so. Be sure you are within the funder's grant range. If you haven't settled on a budget, suggest that you would like to discuss the scope of the project, if the funder is interested.

Should you follow-up with a phone call? This is a matter of personal preference. If your letter says you will follow-up with a call, be sure to do it. If you feel more comfortable waiting for a return letter, that's okay too.

FIGURE 7-1   A Sample Prospecting Letter . . .

AMERICAN LIBRARY ASSOCIATION   50 EAST HURON STREET   CHICAGO, ILLINOIS 60611-2795   U.S.A.
312-944-6780   800-545-2433

April 30, 1987

Mr. Jay Edward Hall
Readers Digest Foundation
Pleasantville, NY 10570

Dear Mr. Hall:

The American Library Association is planning a campaign to develop new generation of readers and prevent the problem of adult functional illiteracy. The national awareness campaign will encourage parents to giv their children a wonderful gift that's free--a public library card.

We are accepting the challenge offered by Secretary of Education William Bennett in his report on elementary education, FIRST LESSONS: "Children should belong to the public library. There is one within striking distance of practically everybody. Let's have a national campaign: ...every child should obtain a library card--and use it."

With proven ability to organize our network of public and school libraries, the American Library Association is seeking funds to support th development of materials for the library card campaign. We'd like to mail a kit of campaign posters, bookmarks, camera ready ads, case studies, letters to parents and more to at least 50,000 public and school libraries All materials will be produced in Spanish and in English. This grassroots campaign will then be supported with national public service advertising, and production funds are needed for radio, television and print public service announcements.

We have better experience at creating materials to promote reading and libraries than at raising funds. Samples of our work are enclosed. The posters we produce help libraries increase their visiblity and gain public support. Since they are distributed on a cost recovery basis, they tend to be used by libraries that can afford them. We see the library car campaign as an opportunity to mobilize every library to reach all parents of elementary school children. Our message is important and the time is right.

We have developed tentative budgets for the campaign. We would lik to submit a proposal to the Readers Digest Foundation, if there is interes

We appreciate your consideration and look forward to hearing from you.

Sincerely,

Thomas J. Galvin
Executive Director

... And The Response

READER'S DIGEST FOUNDATION

PLEASANTVILLE, N.Y. 10570

J. EDWARD HALL
Vice President and
Executive Director

May 11, 1987

Mr. Thomas J. Galvin
American Library Association
50 East Huron Street
Chicago, Illinois 60611

Dear Mr. Galvin:

Thank you for your recent letter regarding the national
awareness campaign to enable every child to obtain a library
card -- and use it.

The problem of adult functional illiteracy is a major one and
of concern to us. Therefore, we would be interested in
receiving a proposal. I am not in a position to make a
commitment but I can assure you that it would be seriously
reviewed.

Thank you for your interest in the Reader's Digest Foundation.

Sincerely,

J. Edward Hall

JEH:mt
229

For some funders, your one or two page letter may take the place of a proposal. For others, a meeting—if you can get one—may be more effective than a letter.

THE PROPOSAL: BASIC COMPONENTS

There are many books about how to write proposals. We especially recommend *Program Planning and Proposal Writing*, a brochure with plenty of examples by Norton J. Kiritz.

Often too much emphasis is put on proposal writing. Your idea and success in catching a potential funder's interest are just as important as the formal proposal. So rather than being intimidated by the task of writing a proposal, think of it as the next logical step toward funding. Writing the proposal helps you think through every part of the project, so your plan becomes perfectly clear. When your project is funded, much of the work will already be done.

There are basic elements that most funders expect to see in a proposal. The following are based on the general elements suggested by Norton Kiritz:

SUMMARY: The cover page of your proposal should include a one paragraph abstract that clearly and concisely summarizes the request, including the total budget request. Write this last, after you have completed all other parts of the proposal.

Introduction: Describe your library's qualifications and establish credibility and context for the grant project.

Statement of the Problem: Document in a compelling manner, the needs to be met or problem to be solved.

Goals and Objectives: Goals are broad, visionary statements of program purpose. Most projects will have only one, or at most two or three goals. Objectives clarify the goals in measurable terms, and clearly establish the benefits of the funding.

Methods: Describe the plan of work; specific strategies that will achieve the stated goals and objectives. It is usually helpful to follow the narrative with a timetable showing when the work will be accomplished within the grant period.

Evaluation: Describe how you will determine whether the project goals and objectives are met.

Future Funding: Explain how the project will be continued after the grant period.

Budget: Clearly show all the costs to be met by the funding source, but also include the costs your library will support, either in-kind or from other funding sources.

Addenda: You may also include appendixes with resumes of key personnel, letters of support, or other relevant background information.

Don't overload your proposal with appendixes.

PROPOSAL WRITING HINTS

Most suggestions about proposal writing are pure common sense. Here are a few reminders:

- Readability is the goal. Use clear, plain English. Avoid jargon and acronyms. Use active rather than passive voice. Keep paragraphs short. Use headings and subheadings.
- Write your proposal with the people who will be served in mind. Talk about their needs and how your library's action will help.
- Be positive. You are describing a great idea and opportunity for the funder. You are not begging.
- Avoid overkill. Charts, graphs, footnotes, and pages of statistics may interrupt your clear narrative.
- Ask someone outside your planning group to read your proposal for understandability and clarity.
- Number your pages and if the proposal is long—more than ten pages—provide a table of contents.
- Use a clear typeface, and make sure the proposal has spacing and margins that make it clear and easy to read. Fancy bindings are not necessary.

- If the funder has a deadline, don't even think about missing it.
- If the funder has an application form or guidelines, follow them to the letter.
- Submit your proposal with a brief cover letter addressed to a specific individual. If you don't know the name of the person who will receive your proposal, you shouldn't have written it.

PROPOSAL CHECKLIST

Please read this checklist when you start your first draft, then come back to it when you're ready to submit your proposal.

1. Have you confirmed that the funding source is interested in receiving your proposal?
2. Have the people you plan to serve been involved in planning the project? Does your proposal reflect their involvement?
3. Does your proposal include information on other individuals or organizations already working on the problem? Have you identified any local partners?
4. If the funding source provides guidelines, have you followed them carefully?
5. Have you covered the basic proposal elements outlined earlier in this chapter?
6. Have you highlighted innovative features of your project that may set it apart from others?
7. Has a draft been read by an impartial outsider for clarity and understanding?
8. Has the budget been reviewed by your organization's fiscal agent? Are the budget items complete? Is the arithmetic correct? Are all budget items explained in the budget notes or the program narrative?
9. Has the narrative been proofread? Are you positive there are no typos?
10. Has the proposal been approved by your board or chief administrative officer?
11. Have copies been distributed to partner organizations or other project participants?

12. Have all copies of the proposal or cover letter been signed by the library director or other official, as your internal procedures require?
13. How many copies of the proposal does the funding agency want?
14. Are you meeting the funder's deadline?

If you've diligently followed all 14 steps listed above, you should have a good chance of getting your project funded. Nevertheless, we all know that not every good proposal is automatically approved; and not every proposal is good. Following are some common errors. They are the flip-side of the basics of grant project development. Having gotten this far, you are surely ready to avoid these errors!

WHY PROPOSALS FAIL

1. The funder did not request the proposal. It was submitted "over the transom" without even an initial letter of intent.
2. The client group the project claims to serve was not involved in developing the project plans.
3. The statement of the problem is not convincing or well documented.
4. The proposal is poorly written, confusing, difficult to follow.
5. The objectives are not within the interests of the funding source.
6. The funder does not know the capabilities of the applicant organization and the proposal does not provide convincing documentation.
7. The applicant has not indicated whether the project will be coordinated with others in the same area of interest.
8. The goals and objectives appear unrealistic or overly ambitious.
9. The budget is unrealistic or incomplete.
10. The budget is beyond the range of the funding agency.
11. The proposal does not follow the funding agency's guidelines.
12. The planned evaluation procedures are insufficient or unconvincing.
13. There is no indication that the project can be sustained beyond the funding period.

VITAL PERSONAL CONTACTS

The person you work with at a foundation, government agency, or corporation will be the key to the success of your project. Once you have a contact, establishing a relationship is important. It can also be frustrating. One of ALA's grant project directors swears that a program officer will make you cry at least once, before a project is funded. Why the stress? Establishing any working relationship is difficult. Program officers don't automatically understand libraries and librarians. They may not talk or think like us. The program officer's job is to help you, but also to be sure that the agency's funds are being invested in an efficient and effective organization. You and your ideas are on trial. It often takes time to come to common ground and mutual understanding. It's all part of the process.

Funders are not passive dispensers of cash. Their organizations have specific goals and philosophies. They want to be involved in shaping the projects they fund. You should be a very good listener, be flexible, and be positive. The confidence you display will help convince the program officer that your library is a good risk. Be willing to participate in planning meetings. Prepare a draft program outline and be prepared to revise and refine it. Be open to suggestions. The project will ultimately be improved by a partnership approach. If a proposal is developed with the help of a program officer, it is more likely to be recommended to the foundation board for funding.

8 FOLLOWING THROUGH

After you have submitted your proposal, it is okay to follow up—in fact, it is important to follow up.

- Call or write the program officer to make sure your proposal was received, and received on time.
- Ask if they need additional information.
- Ask when you might expect to hear from them.
- Don't ask for a meeting. Some foundations may suggest one, or a visit. It is better to respond to their invitation than suggest it yourself.
- Put yourself in the program officer's shoes—he or she is probably overworked and buried in proposals. Constant phone calls or communication from applicants can drive a person crazy. You should be helpful, available to answer questions, and above all, patient.

HOORAY—YOU'RE FUNDED!

First, thank the funder! An acceptance and thank you letter signed by the library director and/or board chair is in order.

Then celebrate! There are few moments that feel this good. Plan a party or reception. Enjoy yourself and invite everyone who helped—it's a great way to share the glory and say thanks!

PLANNING PUBLICITY

After the party, plan the announcement of the grant, developing a publicity plan with the funder. Draft a news release—and be sure to clear it with the funding agency. They may prefer a joint release. Be sure to include quotes from important people—your board chair, the foundation president, a local partner organization representative, and "just folks," the people in the community who will benefit from the project. A sample news release is shown in Figure 8-1.

Develop a project fact sheet with more detail about your project than you included in the news release. Fact sheets are always helpful back up. Writing them helps you organize your thoughts. If you want the press to get the facts straight, give them straight facts. A sample project fact sheet is shown in Figure 8-2.

If the project is really big, consider a press conference, with prepared remarks from the library director, board chair, and the funder. Remember—really big. A press conference ignored by the press will embarrass your boss and the funder.

Release the grant information to the local media (including radio and television), and don't forget the library press. News of

FIGURE 8-1   Sample News Release

**Brooklyn
Public
Library**

News

For Release :   BROOKLYN PUBLIC LIBRARY AWARDED $73,063
                  GRANT TO PURCHASE FOREIGN LANGUAGE MATERIALS
Contact :
                  Donald Kaplan (718) 780-7839

The 2.3 million people served by the Brooklyn

Public Library represent the most ethnically diverse

community in the United States. Ninety-four different

languages are spoken in the borough and over half of

the population speaks English as a second language.

In recognition of Brooklyn's cultural richness and

the importance of a library's ability to meet the

reading needs of the community it serves, the U.S.

Department of Education recently awarded the Brooklyn

Public Library a $73,063 grant under the Foreign

Language Materials Acquisition Program, Title V of the

Library Services and Construction Act. It is the

(continued)

Grand Army Plaza
Brooklyn, New York 11238

FIGURE 8-1   Sample News Release, Cont.

second largest of the 31 grants awarded, and the money
will be used to purchase approximately 10,437 new
fiction and non-fiction books in Spanish, French,
Creole, and Chinese.

"An immigrant's success in adjusting to American
culture depends greatly on the ability to read and
write English," says Ellen Loughran,
coordinator of the office of public service support at
the Brooklyn Public Library. "By providing books in
their native tongue, the library hopes to encourage new
Americans to use the library and eventually make use of
all its books and services, including the Education Job
Information Center, Literacy programs, RIF story hours,
and eventually citizenship materials."

At present the Central Library has books in 80
different languages, including Arabic, Chinese, French,
German, Hebrew, Hungarian, Italian, Polish, Russian,
Spanish, and Yiddish. Nevertheless branch librarians
continue to express a need for additional materials to
meet the huge demand. Nineteen of the library's 58
branches serve Spanish-speaking communities, 14 have
need for French and Creole materials, and 17 serve
Chinese-speaking communities.

November 27, 1991

FIGURE 8-2   Sample Project Fact Sheet

AMERICAN LIBRARY ASSOCIATION

PUBLIC INFORMATION OFFICE
50 EAST HURON STREET   CHICAGO, ILLINOIS 60611
312-944-6780   800-545-2433

FACT SHEET

"Seeds of Change": A Traveling Exhibition

WHO:
The American Library Association, Smithsonian Institution, Federation of State Humanities Councils, National Endowment for the Humanities, and 60 libraries--at least one in every state.

WHAT:
"Seeds of Change": A Traveling Exhibition, based on the major exhibition at the Smithsonian Institution National Museum of Natural History, October 1991-April 1993.

Using five "seeds"--corn, disease, sugar, the potato, and the horse--as case studies, "Seed of Change" explores the global changes, both good and bad, set in motion by Columbus' voyages 500 years ago.

This portable 30-panel exhibition will provide a catalyst for public discussion in communities where it is shown. The host libraries will offer related programs such as lectures, film series, reading and discussion programs.

WHERE:
Public libraries in every state: See itinerary.

WHEN:
A two-year tour: Four copies of the exhibition will travel simultaneously to reach 60 sites for a month each between January 1992 and December 1993.

WHY:
The Columbus Quincentenary provides an opportunity and focus for discussion and education about the global changes of the last 500 years. Libraries provide a community forum, through their vast resources and the programming that interprets these resources for the public.

With a major grant from the National Endowment for the Humanities and additional funding from Beneficial Management Corporation, the American Library Association is collaborating with the Smithsonian Institution Traveling Exhibition Service to bring the scholarship of a major exhibition at the National Museum of Natural History to communities throughout the country.

CONTACT:
Press inquiries:
Pamela Goodes, Linda Wallace, ALA, 312-280-5043, 5042
Liz Hill, SITES, 202-357-4324
Library inquiries: Deb Robertson, 312-280-5057

FIGURE 8-2   Sample Project Fact Sheet, Cont.

SEEDS OF CHANGE
ITINERARY
December 1991

TOUR DATES	TOUR I	TOUR II	TOUR III	TOUR IV
4 Jan-2 Feb 92	Anchorage ALASKA	Bismarck* NORTH DAKOTA	Portland MAINE	Miami FLORIDA
22 Feb-22 Mar 92	Seattle WASHINGTON	Rapid City SOUTH DAKOTA	Derry NEW HAMPSHIRE	Ft.Lauderdale FLORIDA
11 Apr-10 May 92	Salem* OREGON	Omaha NEBRASKA	Montpelier* VERMONT	Birmingham ALABAMA
30 May-4 July 92	San Francisco CALIFORNIA	Kansas City KANSAS	Boston MASSACHUSETTS	Atlanta GEORGIA
18 July-16 Aug 92	Sacramento CALIFORNIA	St.Louis MISSOURI	Columbus OHIO	Georgetown S.CAROLINA
5 Sept-4 Oct 92	Los Angeles CALIFORNIA	Little Rock* ARKANSAS	Providence RHODE ISLAND	Charlotte N.CAROLINA
24 Oct-22 Nov 92	Honolulu* HAWAII	New Orleans LOUISIANA	Buffalo NEW YORK	Richmond* VIRGINIA
12 Dec 92-10 Jan 93	Phoenix ARIZONA	Houston TEXAS	Jamaica NEW YORK	Charleston* W.VIRGINIA
30 Jan-28 Feb 93	Salt Lake Cty UTAH	Dallas TEXAS	Norristown PENNSYLVANIA	Wilmington. DELAWARE
20 Mar-18 Apr 93	Reno NEVADA	Oklahoma Cty OKLAHOMA	Pittsburgh PENNSYLVANIA	Washington D.C.
3 May-6 June 93	Boise IDAHO	Des Moines IOWA	Detroit MICHIGAN	Baltimore MARYLAND
26 June-25 July 93	Billings MONTANA	Minneapolis MINNESOTA	Hartford* CONNECTICUT	Manalapan NEW JERSEY
14 Aug-12 Sept 93	Cheyenne WYOMING	Wis. Rapids WISCONSIN	Louisville KENTUCKY	PUERTO RICO
2 Oct-31 Oct 93	Boulder COLORADO	Chicago ILLINOIS	Knoxville TENNESSEE	St. Croix* U.S.V.I.
20 Nov-26 Dec 93	Albuquerque NEW MEXICO	Indianapolis INDIANA	Vicksburg MISSISSIPPI	St. Croix* U.S.V.I.

*All sites are public libraries, except in cities marked with an asterisk,
where the site is the state library or other state building.

your success may inspire other librarians. Discuss your press list with the funding agency. They will undoubtedly have other news outlets to recommend.

Extend the publicity plan to the whole life of the project. You are probably doing something new and exciting with your grant project. Be sure people know about it. If it was important enough to receive funding, your project is important enough to capture public attention. Publicity will serve the interests of the funder and the library. Even the big, established foundations—even the federal government—like positive publicity. Can you think of any organization that doesn't? Worksheet 8-1 will help you organize your publicity planning.

If your project has an advisory committee, ask the funder to participate as a full-standing member of the committee. The best projects are partnerships, and we guarantee you will benefit from the funder's perspective. If full participation isn't of interest to the funder, you may still want to invite your program officer to attend key meetings.

Be sure to acknowledge the funder in any publicity and on all materials—including letterhead—developed for or about the project. This sounds so obvious, but it is too often forgotten. You should develop a credit line, clear it with the funder and use it consistently. For example: "My Mom and Me" is a partnership project of the Cabell County Public Library and the Bell Atlantic Charitable Foundation.

REPORTING AND EVALUATION

Set up procedures to carefully monitor grant funds. Some foundations pay out grant funds with one or two checks during the life of the project. Others, such as the National Endowment for the Humanities establish "draw-down" procedures that enable the recipient to receive payments as the grant funds are needed. Whatever the payment plan, you will be required to provide a financial report.

Find out immediately about all reporting requirements. Be prepared to meet the reporting deadlines. It is helpful to review the evaluation plans developed in your proposal and make sure you are ready to do what you promised.

In addition to quantitative evaluation, collect anecdotes and quotes from people your project serves. This material is invaluable for developing more proposals, for developing good publicity, and for writing meaningful reports. Photographs are also extremely helpful, especially if they tell a story or capture the human value of your project.

WORKSHEET 8-1

PUBLICITY/PROMOTION IDEA SHEET

	Internal	*External*
Newspapers		
Radio		
Television		
Speeches		
Special Publications		
Direct Contacts		
Exhibits and Displays		
Special Events		
Others		

Continue to maintain a good relationship with the funder. Keep in touch. Meet all your deadlines. The surest way to establish yourself with a funding agency is to do an excellent job of carrying out the grant project. Keep the funder informed and involved. If you produce printed materials for the project, send copies to the funder.

Your performance on the first project with a funder will quickly establish your reputation. We've heard that in days gone by, many foundations would provide continuous funding to chosen organizations. With the current emphasis on funding specific projects to solve specific problems, no one can count on "automatic" funding. Even so, if you do an excellent job of meeting your project goals, future funding is possible, and you will also be recommended to other funders. The world of corporate and foundation giving is almost as small as the library world. We assure you—program officers talk with one another.

Think about the final report at the beginning of the project rather than the end. Thankfully, most funders are more interested in the work you do with grant funds than they are in reports. But a final report is essential, even if the funder doesn't require one. A final report will give you the opportunity to consider whether you met your goals—whether the grant project was a worthwhile investment of your time, the library's resources, and the funders money. Be sure to find out immediately what is required and when it is due. You might also ask to see copies of good final reports.

At ALA we have developed a method for final reports on major grants from the National Endowment for the Humanities that provides us with a useful record of the project and satisfies the reporting requirement. We combine the evaluation and final narrative report in a scrapbook with samples of all the project materials and publicity—even letters from participants. We produce three copies of the book; one for NEH, one for our library, and one for use in our offices. This plodding method pulls together all the pieces of a big project and has proven to be well worth the time invested.

OH, NO

You didn't get the grant. Don't be too discouraged. And don't give up. Only about one in ten proposals is funded, so you're in good company. If you have followed all the recommended steps to this point, you now have some major accomplishments—a well-conceived and carefully planned project and some important new contacts. Make use of your accomplishments.

Ask the program officer (one of your new contacts) why your proposal was not funded. You can also ask if it should be submitted again, or whether he or she can recommend other sources. Some program officers may even volunteer to call other foundations on your behalf.

Some granting agencies, such as the National Endowment for the Humanities, have written comments from all the panel members who read and reviewed your proposal. You can ask to receive these written comments. The federal agencies such as NEH are required to give you panelist's comments upon request, or you may file a Freedom of Information inquiry. Private foundations do not have this obligation. With NEH, it is especially important to try again. Ask for suggestions. Improve the proposal and resubmit. Many NEH grants are awarded on second and third tries. As Tom Phelps of NEH commented in the interview in chapter 4, almost 90 percent of resubmissions to the NEH library program are funded.

If you have generated great enthusiasm for your project you should consider seeking other sources, or even meeting with staff and board members to decide if there is a way the project—or even a few of the inspired ideas—can be launched without grant funding.

REALITY CHECK

INTERVIEW WITH WICKY SLEIGHT

If you think a small library with few staff members couldn't possibly seek and win grant support, you're wrong. The following interview with Wicky Sleight, Director of the Marshall Missouri Public Library will show you how it *can* be done.

Q: *Your library has received several grants; can you give us a quick sketch of your library and community?*

A: The library is two years old. We're open 69 hours a week, and serve a population of 12,000. I am the only full-time staff person and the only professional librarian. I do reference, cataloging, selection, planning, budgeting—everything but janitorial. We have three part-time staff members. So far, we have 20,000 volumes and our circulation is almost 8,000 per month. Developing grant projects is one of the most important things I do. It is definitely a priority.

Q: *What grants have you received?*

A: We have received five LSCA Title I grants, an NEH *Voices & Vision* grant from ALA, also an NEH *Poets in Person* from ALA. We have had two Ezra Jack Keats mini-grants. From the Missouri Humanities Council we've received grants for a film series on American values, and supplementary funds to double the honorarium for our *Poets in Person* scholar plus $860 for program promotion. (An Ezra Jack Keats mini-grant proposal and an LSCA proposal are shown in Appendix F.)

Q: *Have they had a positive benefit?*

A: I write a lot of press releases. The grants are positive news about what our new library is doing. Each program is different. They attract different people, many who have never been in the library. For example, one Ezra Jack Keats grant was for materials for parents and care givers—a good target audience for us. The grants help us get people in from other little towns and will eventually, I think, help us expand our tax base. But if they just walk in the door, that's important to me. This year I've written an LSCA proposal for health materials. We'll find out about it in June.

Q: *How did you hear about these opportunities?*

A: I find out about most of them in library literature. I also have all the foundation directories. So many foundations fund only in their state. Missouri now has a new local directory that will help me a lot. When I think I have a lead—maybe a local branch of a national company—I'll call the local president and tell him or her I'd like to talk about getting some money for the library. Usually the company president is in Rotary—I'm in Rotary. The library pays my dues. A local company, Con Agra, makes frozen dinners. I'm going to approach them with a proposal for computer-assisted adult learning. They have three shifts of unskilled workers. I think the idea may be of interest to them.

Q: *How do you find time to do the proposals?*

A: They are a top priority. It helps to have deadlines. I write on work time, though I may think and plan on off hours. I think about the funders and what their needs are. Sometimes it helps just to walk around and think about the ideas.

Q: *Do you apply for a lot of grants that are not funded?*

A: I wrote what I thought was a great proposal in response to an RFP I saw in a journal from the Lois Lenski Corey Foundation, and never heard a word. But I'll use it again. A couple of my LSCA proposals weren't funded, but I usually know when the losers are losers.

Q: *How does the staff feel abut your grant activity?*

A: The staff is proud. They don't think it is just more work for them. We're number *one*. In fact, we applied for library of the year! I do a lot of brainstorming with the staff.

Q: *Have your projects received good press coverage and good community support?*

A: Absolutely. I always send press releases to the state library and state library association as well as the local press. They all give us good coverage. I'm trying to get more librarians in Missouri to do humanities programming. It's frustrating. I guess they think they are just caretakers. We get good turnout for our programs. We had more than 25 people for the *Poets in Person* discussion series.

Q: *Have you done the public library planning process? Do you have a mission statement?*

A: We have not done the planning process. We do have a mission statement, but I don't often use it in proposals. Our board is not interested in planning. They have made it very clear that the priority is programs.

Q: *What is the most difficult thing about applying for grants?*

A: Getting started. It's like starting to write or creating a poem. You just have to get started. It is also critical that you follow through and administer the grant. I've gotten the Keats grant twice because they know we do a good job. You have to publicize, evaluate, take pictures, submit good reports. It's not easy to spend $20,000, but if you say you're going to do it, you have to do it. And you've got to do it just they way they tell you. Don't argue with them. I worked for the state government for 17 years, so I know I have to do it the way they want.

Q: *What is your advice to librarians who have never applied for a grant?*

A: Just know that you can do it! Some proposals will be rejected, but if it's a good idea you can use it somewhere else. The project has to be part of the mission of the library. It has to fill a need. Always take advantage of any offer to critique. I always have someone read my proposals who doesn't have a stake in the project, and I almost always make the changes they suggest. It's also important to do a lot of research. Do literature searches. I use Wilsonline. For example if I'm considering a project on health information I'll see what other libraries are doing. I guess the best advice is to just go ahead and do it!

CONCLUSION

We conclude this collection of advice for grant seekers by echoing the encouragement from successful librarians like Georgia Lomax and Wicky Sleight, "Just know that you can do it! Just do it!" While grant funds should never replace local tax support for public libraries, there are funds available that will help you enhance services and launch new services. Furthermore the process of seeking grants is a healthy and productive exercise.

If you have read or browsed all the way through this book, the next thing you should do is get a copy of the *Foundation Center's User Friendly Guide*, talk to people in your community who have successfully pursued grants, keep an eye on library literature for grant opportunities, think positive, and just do it!

APPENDIX A:

FLATHEAD COUNTY LIBRARY
MACARTHUR GRANT APPLICATION

GRANT APPLICATION FORM
(All sections should be completed within the space provided)

I. YOUR LIBRARY

1. Applicant

   Name of Library: FLATHEAD COUNTY LIBRARY

   Address: 247 First Ave. East; Kalispell, MT 59901

   Contact Person: Georgia Lomax, Director   Phone: 406/756-5688

2. Does your library have any branch locations? How many? ___4___ Branch(es)
   (If none, enter "0")

3. Does your library have a circulating video collection? How many videotapes does it
   have? ___43___ Videotapes   (if none, enter 0)

4. Which is the nearest main public library to yours?
   Of comparable size:
   NAME __Missoula Public Library__

   CITY Missoula, MT _____ DISTANCE ___110___ Miles

   Nearest larger library is in Spokane, Washington --

II. SIZE OF POPULATION SERVED

Please provide information for the combined total of your main library and any branches.

1. For what geographic area is your library the primary public library?

   Name of Area __Flathead County (5112 square miles)__

   Census Population of Area (Current Estimate)__57,800 (7/1/86 estimate)__

2. Approximately, how many patrons come into your main library (and any branches)
   per week? ___4040___

3. What is the average number of books checked out (main and any branches) each
   week? ___7791___

4. If you have a video collection, what is the average number of videotapes checked out
   (main and any branches) each week? ___10___ (Check out period is 10 days, which
   reduces circulation figures, but
   allows adequate time to use our current
   nonfiction selection.)

III. TYPE OF GRANT OR OTHER ASSISTANCE REQUESTED

We would like to apply for the following kinds of grant or assistance (Please re-read the eligibility requirements and the criteria for selection before indicating your options; fill in the number for each).

_____ A (1)　　A $1000 matching grant towards the purchase of a $3000 set (A or B).

__X__ A (2)　　A $2000 matching grant towards the purchase of a $6000 set (A and B).

_____ B　　　An outright grant of $3000 set of series B.

_____ C (1)　　An outright grant of a $3000 set of Series A or B as a Main Library with more than 10 branch libraries. Fill in _____ of set _____ .

_____ C (2)　　An outright grant of $3000 towards the purchase of a $6000 set as a Main Library with more than 10 branches.

_____ D (1)　　An outright grant of a $3000 set of Series A or B as a Regional Library System. Fill in _____ of set _____ .

_____ D (2)　　An outright grant of $3000 towards the purchase of a $6000 set (A and B) as a Regional Library System.

_____ E　　　Our Library would like to purchase (fill in the number) _____ 10 series A; _____10 series B; _____ 20 series (A and B) under the three payment interest free purchase program described under "E."

IV. VIDEO CLASSICS OWNERSHIP

How many sets of the Video Classics have already been acquired?

_____ 10 Series Sets

__1__ 20 Series Sets　(We already have ordered our series under the delayed billing option in an earlier letter from Mary Mulvaney.)

V. BUDGET INFORMATION

All applicants should provide the following information for the most recent completed fiscal year (main and any branches):

A. Annual gross budget __$490,047__

B. Annual gross budget for purchase of books __$70,852__

C. Annual gross budget for purchase of videocassettes __$900__

D. Annual gross income from cassette rentals __-0-__

E. Population served __57,800 (7/1/86 census estimates)__

F. Annual per capita* gross budget __$8.47__

G. Annual per capita* budget for books __$1.23__

H. Annual per capita* budget for videocassettes __2¢__

* per capita budget computed by dividing the gross budget by the estimated 1987 census population of the area served by the library

VI. CHARACTERISTICS OF POPULATION SERVED

Please check any of the groups below which make up a substantial proportion of the population served by your library. Where possible, indicate the approximate percentage that each group represents among:

a) The population of your area
b) Your library's patrons

☐ BLACK	a _____ %	b _____ %
☐ HISPANIC	a _____ %	b _____ %
XX NATIVE AMERICAN	a __1__ %	b __1__ %
☐ PRIMARILY SPEAKING A FOREIGN LANGUAGE (Not fluent in English)	a _____ %	b _____ %
XX OVER THE AGE OF 65	a __30__ %	b __40__ %

What other special characteristics, if any, of the community served by your library should be taken into consideration?

Flathead County has a population of 57,800 (7/1/86 census estimates) spread across an area nearly twice as large as the states of Rhode Island and Delaware combined. It is for the most part rural. Severe weather, poor roads, and geography keep residents confined to the local area for much of the year. Nearest educational centers are in Missoula, MT, three hours drive south, and Spokane, WA, two states away. The beauty and isolation of the rugged Flathead Valley has drawn many people seeking to escape the problems of busy cities, and those who wish to return to nature or a simpler lifestyle. The area's economy is primarily supported by the short tourism season and by logging, an industry that has faced severe problems recently. Many residents are employed only seasonally. In 1980, the unemployment rate for the county was 13 percent. It has continued to remain above state and national averages during this decade of closures and cutbacks for local employers.

The Library provides service through 5 library outlets. It also serves Swan River Forest Camp (a residential corrections facility for men), Montana Veterans' Home, day cares, and nursing and retirement homes. A homebound service is being developed. The Library circulated nearly 7 items per capita in FY88, with statistics showing that each person in the county would have used the Library 1.3 times during that period. The Library provided 368 educational programs during FY88, which were VII. NEEDS ASSESSMENT attended by 7231 community members (nearly 20 people per program)

Explain why you need financial assistance. Refer to the factors on page 3 of the guideline letter applicable to the category for which you have applied.

Despite poor economic conditions, residents of Flathead County have supported the Library as much as possible. However, money is limited (in taxes and in individual donations) and must be spread among many deserving causes. The book budget has been maintained at a level that allows adequate basic operation and collection maintenance for the five outlets in the County. It does not allow the development of new collections. Purchase of the video classics series will establish a video collection which the Library budget can maintain and build.

The Library system plays an active and visible role in the business and cultural community, and seeks to respond to local needs, concerns and interests. While rental stores provide many video offerings, they are unable to provide quality non-fiction or cultural material as it does not support itself financially. The Library feels there is a demand for this material, and it is an appropriate service to be offered through the Library.

PBS offerings are available only via cable TV subscription in Flathead County. Cable access is limited by location (must be near the three cities in the county). Approximately 53% of county households are within cable boundaries, though currently only about 42% subscribe. Those who cannot afford the service, or who are outside boundaries are unable to receive the PBS channel from Spokane, WA.

VII. NEEDS ASSESSMENT (continued)

If applying for assistance under category A, please rate your prospects for providing matching funds:

XX Excellent   ☐ Good   ☐ Fair

*Have raised $1000 from the community, fund drive continues. The Library will contribute as much as possible, as well.

VIII. CIRCULATION COMMITMENT

Describe what commitment you will make if you receive a grant or other assistance, to promote the circulation, outreach and promotion of the Video Classics. Applicants for CATEGORY C please state how they will place and use cassettes.

CIRCULATION: All segments of the series' will be available for checkout at no cost to the patron. (Video use policy attached). Thye will also be entered in the Western Library Network database and thus available to patrons of other libraries through interlibrary loan service.

OUTREACH: The video classics will be available to patrons through any library outlet, and the collection will be rotated among the branches and institutions served. The Library maintains a close working relationship with the rural and city schools, the local community college (the public library is its library), the Montana Veterans' Home, Swan River Forest Camp, retirement/ nursing homes, county jail, group homes, etc., and will make them available. All will be informed that they are here.

PROMOTION: The series will continually be promoted. Local media are extremely cooperative in informing the community of library services through PSAs and articles. The series' will be highlighted in all talks to community groups and in tours given. A fund raising project is currently underway, and is also being used as an advertising device to inform the community. Videos are prominently displayed near the front door and check out area to catch the eye of library users. The Library also provides an adult literacy program, and the videos will be tied into its teaching as well.

The Library provides many free programs to the community. The video series will be used on a continuing basis as a regular program feature -- providing an audience and advertising of the resource. This should generate demand and circulation.

Are you willing to submit a summary of your circulation and programming of the Classics by December 31, 1989?

XX Yes   ☐ No

Signature of Authorizing Official: _Georgia Lomax_____

Print Name:____Georgia Lomax_____

Title:_____Director_____

Mail to:

The John D. and Catherine T. MacArthur Foundation
Library Video Classics Project
P.O. Box 409113
Chicago, IL 60640

We would appreciate prompt submission of this application.

FLATHEAD COUNTY LIBRARY

247 First Avenue East

Kalispell, Montana

59901

Columbia Falls Branch
59912

Whitefish Branch
59937

Phone: 752-5300 Ext. 357

APPROVED
10/22/87

VIDEO CASSETTE POLICY

The Board of Trustees of the Flathead County Library recognizes that information and entertainment is available in many forms. FCL will provide resources in non-traditional forms for the community it serves whenever appropriate and possible.

The Board acknowledges that private enterprises are legitimate agencies for resource sharing practices and shall strive to limit duplication within the entire community of resource sources. It is not the Board's intention to compete with private sector operations.

CHECKOUT

Loan period -- 10 days.

Limit -- one tape per person.

Overdue fine -- $1 first day; $3 second day; $5/day for third day and each thereafta

Tape must be rewound before being returned.

Reserves may be placed on videos. Patrons may not place reserves for specific dates.

ELIGIBLE BORROWERS

Patrons must have a valid library card to borrow video tapes.

New library card applicants must show current identification before being allowed to borrow videos.

Patrons must complete a responsibility card before checking out video cassettes. Patrons under 18 years of age must have a parent or guardian sign the card in the presence of library staff.

PARENTAL RESPONSIBILITY

In compliance with FCL's policy to not restrict access to information due to age, all patrons meeting the above requirements may borrow tapes with no restrictions. Library staff shall not monitor use of video tapes.

The Board declares that it is the responsibility of the family to monitor a minor's selection of video tapes, as it is with all other library materials; and to determine and enforce family viewing standards. A parent/guardian's signature on a minor's responsibility card acknowledges their agreement to accept full responsibility in this matter.

SELECTION

Selection of video tapes shall be made according to the same criteria applied to all other library materials (see Materials Selection Policy).

COPYRIGHT RESTRICTIONS

The Board of Trustees recognizes that stringent copyright restrictions apply to information and entertainment available on video cassette. In order to comply with these restrictions, copyrighted videos will be provided for a patron's home use only.

No copyrighted video may be copied under any circumstance.

VOICES & VISIONS

Reading, viewing and discussion
programs in America's Libraries

**Application form
Voices & Visions Project**

FLATHEAD COUNTY LIBRARY
Name of library

247 - 1st Ave. East
Address

Kalispell,   MT   59901
City   State   Zip

406 - 756-5690
Phone

Joyce G. Johnson, Head, Public Services
Name and title of staff person to be in charge of Voices & Visions Project

• Tell us about your library (size and make-up of the community, special
populations served, library community activities, etc.):

Please see attached narrative.

• What is your target audience for this program (e.g., young adults, young
mothers, senior citizens, prison population, inner city residents, rural
residents)? Why?

Please see attached narrative.

• What experience has your library had with presenting humanities programming (e.g., participation in the Let's Talk About It project)?

Please see attached narrative.

_____

_____

_____

_____

• What kinds of support can you draw on for this program (state library, state humanities council, local scholars, friends of the library, local poetry group, etc.)? You are encouraged to send a letter of support from any of these groups with your application.

Please see attached narrative.

_____

_____

_____

_____

In what ways will they provide assistance?

Please see attached narrative and letters of support.

_____

We hereby apply to be a demonstration library in the "Voices & Visions: Reading, Viewing and Discussion Programs in America's Libraries" project. We agree to provide staff time and a meeting location for an 8- to 10-week program series, as well as support in the promotion of the series.

Library Director _____
Georgia Lomax, Library Director

We hereby endorse the application of the library named above and agree to support their participation through donated time and/or services.

State Agency Representative: _____
(state library, state humanities council or state library association)
Please see attached facsimile with signature of Montana State Librarian.

1. Tell us about your library (size and make-up of the community, special populations served, library community activities, etc.)

Flathead County Library has a population of 57,800, spread across an area nearly twice as large as the states of Rhode Island and Delaware combined (5112 square miles). Library service is provided by the Flathead County Library System through five outlets.

Flathead County is for the most part rural; severe weather, poor roads and geography keep residents confined to the local area for much of the year. The nearest centers of education are in Missoula, Montana, three hours drive to the south and in Spokane, Washington, two states away.

The area's economy is primarily supported by the short tourism season and by logging, an industry facing severe problems. In 1980, the unemployment rate for the county was 13%; it has remained above state and national rates during a decade of closures and cutbacks for many local employers.

The county's population is predominantly white with a small group of Native Americans. Nearly 30% of its residents are age 60 or older and this increases substantially with summer residents each year.

The library system plays an active and visible role in the business and cultural community, and seeks to respond quickly to local needs, concerns and interest. In recent years it has developed a widely used literacy program and has strengthened its commitment to programming as community demands have required. (see attached library program sheets) - Attachment No. 3

The Library circulated nearly 7 items per capita in FY89, with statistics showing that each person in the county would have used the library 1.3 times during that period. The Library presented nearly 400 programs during FY89 which were attended by 7500 community members (an average of nearly 20 people per program).

The Library also serves the Swan River Forest Camp, a residential corrections facility for men, and the Montana Veterans' Home, as well as day care centers and nursing and retirements homes. A service to the homebound has been developed in one outlet at this time.

2. What is your target audience for this program (e.g., young adults, young mothers, senior citizens, prison population, inner city residents, rural residents)? Why?

This project will target primarily the senior citizens and the young adults in our community. Bringing these two diverse groups together will allow the Library staff to foster an enthusiasm for poetry among community members. and bring together people with different backgrounds and perspectives to share poetry from each one's unique outlook.

Both age groups have been identified as "underserved" by the Library and emphasis during the next year will be placed on seeking ways to better serve their needs. This program will be a part of a larger attempt to upgrade service.

Voices and Visions II   page 2

Census estimates place nearly one-third of Flathead County's population over age 60. Nearly 20% are young adults within the Library's target range for this program(age 16 - 25 years).

This program will be continued and expanded to make it available to more community members by offering future sessions and "taking it on the road" to nursing and retirement homes and to institutions served by the Library.

3. What experience has your library had with presenting humanities programming (e.g. participation in the Let's Talk About It project)?

The Board of Trustees and staff of the Flathead County Library are committed to providing programming for community members.

The Library's mission is to provide informational, educational and entertainment resources for the community in any appropriate format. FCL adds the non-permanent format of "local experts" to the usual formats embraced by libraries, such as videos, books and software.

The Library identified a need for programming in the community in response to a lack of "free" educational and cultural activities for families with no disposable income. During the 1989 summer's program series, 52 programs were attended by 1,281 people. (see attached brochures for summer 1989 programs as well as other offerings throughout the year). - Attachment No. 3

The Library's program committee plans, organizes and runs the programs. Staff has experience with all aspects of programming -- from developing ideas, to organizing, advertising and running the programs, to providing "support material" (bookmarks, displays, etc.).

During the months of January through April a series of six book discussions through Book Group and our state humanities organization was offered. It was a great success and left participants with a desire for more. (see attached program) - Attachment 3F

4. What kinds of support can you draw on for this program (state library, state humanities countil, local scholars, friends of the library, local poetry group, etc.)? You are encouraged to send a letter of support from any of these groups with your application.

FLATHEAD COUNTY LIBRARY: Oversee the project, provide staff and supplies for planning/promoting/executing the project, organize the team for training and presentation, share its experiences with other libraries and groups in the state and encourage duplication of the project, evaluate the project following the end of the program, encourage an enthusiasm and appreciation of poetry and of developing poetry programming.

FLATHEAD VALLEY COMMUNITY COLLEGE: Library and college have a close working relationship (the public library is the college library). Provide personnel. public relations and advertising in brochures and on signboards and provide classroom facilities for the sessions if needed. (letter of support attached. - Attachment No. 1A

Voices and Visions II   page 3

LOWELL JAEGER: Flathead Valley Community College Humanities Division Chairman.
Work with the library as the humanities scholar (resume attached). -Attachment No. 1

FRIENDS OF FLATHEAD COUNTY LIBRARY: Provide people power as needed, and
financial support if necessary. (letter of support attached). - Attachment No. 1C

LOCAL MEDIA: five newspapers, six radio stations and one television station.
Provide public service announcements and other information about the program.
The Library has an excellent relationship with the local media and always
receives comprehensive coverage.

MONTANA STATE LIBRARY: Provide support as needed, assist in passing
information about the project on to the rest of the state (letter of support
sent directly to project director).

MONTANA COMMITTEE FOR THE HUMANITIES: Provide information and advice as
needed. (letter of support attached). - Attachment No. 1B

5. In what ways will they provide assistance?

Please see section 4 above and letters of support attached.

Voices and Visions II   Page 4

ATTACHMENTS:

1. Letters of support

    A. Flathead Valley Community College
    B. Montana Committee for the Humanities
    C. Friends of Flathead County Library
    D. Montana State Library - sent directly to project director

2. Personal Data Sheet - Lowell Jaeger

3. Program Brochures

    A. We Got There on the Train - Summer, 1989
    B. Circus! - Summer Programs, 1989
    C. Centennial Programs, 1989
    D. Children's Programs, 1989
    E. Adult Programs, Winter, 1990
    F. Book Group, Winter, 1990
    G. Spring Programs, 1990
    H. Summer Safari, 1990

APPENDIX B:

CALIFORNIA STATE LSCA APPLICATION "STAFF TRAINING FOR A MULTICULTURAL ENVIRONMENT"

California State Library
Library Services and Construction Act
Fiscal Year 1991/92
Title I and III

APPLICATION

Submit in four copies by 5 pm, **June 3, 1991** to Attn: Collin Clark, Library Development Services, 1001 Sixth St., Suite 300, Sacramento, CA 95814-3324.

1. Project title: ___Staff Training for a Multicultural Environment___

2. Applicant jurisdiction: ___Peninsula Library System___

    ___25 Tower Rd. San Mateo, CA 94402-4000___

3. Applicant contact: ___Linda Crowe___   Phone: ___415 349 5538___

4. District: Assembly ___19, 20, 21___   State Senate ___8 & 11___   House ___11 & 12___

5. Population: Client ___53,821___   Total ___430,351___

6. LSCA Program Activity ___disadvantaged persons___

7. Participants other than applicant:

Signature	Library/Agency
Beverly J. Brin	Sunnyvale Public Library
Susan A. Fuller	Santa Clara County Library
Elizabeth C. Avee	Santa Clara City Library
Jann Of	Redwood City Public Library
Nancy Lewis	San Mateo County Library
Linda M. Saltzer	Daly City Public Library

8. LSCA amount requested: _____ $103,906

91/92 LSCA 6:1

118

Project Title <u>Staff Training for a Multicultural Environment</u>
Applicant Jurisdiction <u>Peninsula Library System</u>

---

9. Project Summary: complete in space provided.
The goal of this project is to train public service staff to
work effectively with the various multicultural, multiethnic
populations in their community. The training specifically
builds the confidence of staff in participating libraries to
work with patrons from various ethnic backgrounds through use
of a manual that focuses on practical skills as well as
affective techniques.

The specific objectives are:

1. To gather data, input and feedback by working with an
advisory committee representing six participating libraries:
Daly City, Filipino; East Palo Alto, Black; Redwood City,
Hispanic; Santa Clara County, Milpitas Community Library,
Vietnamese; Santa Clara Public Library, Korean; and Sunny-
vale, Chinese.

2. To provide specific feedback by engaging a community consultant from the target population to work with the (6)
participating libraries.

3. To develop a resource manual for training public service
staff in both practical skills and behavioral techniques.

4. To train public service staff in participating libraries
in the practical skills and behavioral techniques to meet the
internal needs of staff who need effective techniques to
serve their diverse and changing populations.

5. To test the skills developed during the training in the
participating libraries.

6. To evaluate the training techniques and the integration of
the skills into staff behavior.

As a model this project has major implications for public
libraries in California. It develops tools that will assist
staff to improve service to the growing multicultural, multiethnic, multilingual communities in the State. As a side
benefit the cooperation between libraries in Peninsula
Library System, San Mateo County and South Bay Cooperative
Library System, Santa Clara County encourages the continuing
relationship between the two systems.

10. Budget Summary:

	LSCA (1)	Other funds (2)	In-kind (3)	Total (4)
a. Salaries & Benefits	43,710	_____	30,000	73,710
b. Library Materials	500	_____	_____	500
c. Operation	50,250	_____	2,000	52,250
d. Equipment	0	0	0	0
e. Indirect Cost	9,446	_____	_____	9,446
f. Total	$103,906	0	$32,000	$135,906

Project Title <u>Staff Training for a Multicultural Environment</u>
Applicant Jurisdiction <u>Peninsula Library System</u>

11. Client needs and project goals.

The Rand Study commissioned by the California State Library reports that "In 1988 40% of the state's population was composed of several minority groups." It also states "that there are fewer minorities among public library users and the general population." Libraries need to meet the challenge of serving diverse growing population groups, but staff often lacks the knowledge and tools to interact effectively with these diverse and growing groups.

The Core training funded by the California State Library focused specifically on improving reference skills and increasing the confidence of the participants in meeting patrons' information needs. The training for working in a multicultural environment builds on the concept of CORE, that is building staff confidence to work with <u>all</u> patrons from varied multicultural, multiethnic backgrounds who will be using the library.

An example might be a person who spoke only Tongan coming to the library for assistance and finding that no one on the staff spoke the language. This is generally viewed by staff and patron as a negative experience, but with appropriate non-verbal training library staff could communicate a positive response. The patron might leave with a feeling that in spite of the language barrier the library is a helpful place and return with a friend or family member who could act as an interpreter.

The specific goal of the project is to train public service staff to work effectively with the various multicultural, multiethnic populations in their communities. This will be accomplished by developing a manual with both practical skills such as useful phrases in other languages, effective public relations and information and referral as well as effective behavioral techniques. This project compliments Partnerships for Change and where appropriate will use materials developed for it.

While Partnerships for Change is designed to analyze and restructure service programs this project develops practical and behavioral skills that will heighten staff ability to provide more effective service. It impacts all levels of staff from director to page and challenges them to focus on <u>all</u> of the people that the library serves.

12. Measurable objective to reach goals.

1. To gather data, input and feedback by working with an advisory committee from six participating libraries: Daly City, Filipino; East Palo Alto, Black; Redwood City, Hispanic; Santa Clara County, Milpitas Community Library, Vietnamese; Santa Clara Public Library, Korean; and Sunnyvale, Chinese.

2. To provide specific feedback by engaging a community consultant from each target population to work with the (6) participating libraries.

3. To develop a resource manual for training public service staff in both practical skills and behavioral techniques.

4. To train public service staff in participating libraries in practical skills and behavioral techniques to meet the internal needs of staff who need effective techniques to serve the diverse and changing population.

5. To test the skills developed during the training in the participating libraries.

6. To evaluate the training techniques and the integration of the skills into staff behavior.

13. Project actions in time sequence

1. To gather data, input and feedback by working with an advisory committee representing six participating libraries: Daly City, Filipino; East Palo Alto, Black; Redwood City, Hispanic; Santa Clara County, Milpitas Community Library, Vietnamese; Santa Clara Public Library, Korean; and Sunnyvale, Chinese.

started during grant-writing ongoing	. six librarians representing the six participating libraries have met and provided guidance to the proposal process (Attachment 1)
August, 1991	. advisory committee meets as focus group to assess specific training needs
October 1991	. committee will interview and select a project director (see personnel section 14 for fuller description)
Oct. 1991 Dec. 1991 March, July,	. advisory committee will meet to assess progress; to work with resource consultant(s); to review manual to evaluate the project results; and to plan for continuation and dissemination.

2. To provide specific feedback by engaging a community consultant to work with the (6) participating libraries.

Oct. 1991	. a representative from the target community of the participating library will interpret the community to the library and the library to the community (see personnel section 14 for fuller description)
	. the advisory committee member from each library and the project director will select the community consultant
Dec. 1991 March 1992 July 1992	. community consultant will meet with advisory committee and project director
June – Aug.	. community consultant will participate in training sessions with library staff
Sept. 1992	. community consultants will meet with project director and advisory board to assess their participation

3. To develop a resource manual for training public service staff in both practical skills and behavioral techniques.

Oct., Nov.,1991   . project director with assistance of resource consultant(s) will identify tools and review materials developed for cross-cultural training eg. Partnerships for Change Manual, the CORE materials for improving reference service to to Hispanics and Asians, and FUENTES, a product from BALIS/BPLG grant.

Nov. 1991 Sept. 1992   . project director will meet regularly with community consultants to integrate community needs into resource manual and training

Dec. 1991 Jan. 1992   . project director will write a draft of resource manual

Feb., March 1992   . resource consultant(s), community consultants, and advisory committee will review draft of manual

April 1992   . project director finalizes manual and has it printed

May 1992   . resource manual is reviewed by participating libraries

4. To train public service staff in participating libraries in practical skills and behavioral techniques to meet the internal needs of staff who need effective techniques to serve their diverse and changing population.

Dec - Feb 1992   . Contact PFC libraries working with same populations, eg. Contra Costa working with Filipinos.

March, April 1992   . resource consultant(s) work with project director, advisory board and community consultants to plan training models

May 1992   . directors from participating libraries will meet for orientation on training and manual

May, June 1992   . resource consultant(s) has training session for advisory committee, project director, and community consultants.

June, July 1992   . resource consultant(s) with assistance from project director and community consultants train staff in participating libraries.

Sept. 1992   . resource manual available in loose leaf binder for use by other interested libraries for training staff

5. To test the skills developed during training in the participating libraries

June, July,   . as staff are trained they begin to incorporate
Aug., Sept.   behavior into work life
1992 ongoing

            . staff and community consultants will observe
incorporation of behavior and discuss at training
or follow-up sessions

6. To evaluate the training techniques and the integration of skills into staff behavior

March thru   . evaluators work with project director and
Sept. 1992   resource consultant(s) to develop evaluation
instruments to be used with resource
manual

Sept. 1992   . evaluators, community consultants and project
director hold focus groups for staff in participating libraries to determine the level of
satisfaction with the training models

            . staff and community consultants will evaluate
their training experience using instruments
developed by evaluators and project director

            . participating staff meet with advisory board
and community consultant to discuss the impact of
the training on attitudinal and behavioral
changes they or colleagues have made as a result
of training

June 1993   . staff participate in nine month evaluation

14. Personnel requirement and staff training.

PROJECT DIRECTOR - full time
Desired Capabilities
- ability to work with people from a wide range of cultural and ethnic backgrounds
- ability to listen, assimilate information and communicate it concisely and clearly
- ability to deal effectively with a broad range of personnel in libraries, agencies and organizations
- ability to translate library needs to resource consultant(s), community consultants and staff in participating libraries
- good oral, written and organizational skills
- flexibility in dealing with a fluid situation

Educational Background
Background in librarianship, education, training or social work. Experience working with various ethnic groups is desirable.

RESOURCE CONSULTANTS 12 days
Consultants: Rafael Gonzales Enterprises (attachment 2)
- advises and assists with resource manual
- focuses on diversity
- builds staff confidence in working with multi cultural, multiethnic, multilingual populations.
- trains staff as trainers for their library

COMMUNITY CONSULTANTS 20 days

A representative living in each of the six participating libraries' service areas representing the target population will act as consultants to the project. They will review the manual as it develops and participate in the staff training. They will assist the project director and resource consultants in interpreting the community to the library and the library to the community. The community consultant should be active in the community with ties to community agencies. Bilingual, where appropriate.

EVALUATOR 115 hours   (attachment 3)
Consultants: ETI
- develops basic design for evaluation
- design instrument for evaluation of training and manual
- designs instrument for testing project effectiveness after nine months

15. Statewide significance.

As a model this project has major implications for public libraries throughout the State. As the Rand report states and the 1990 census confirms, California communities are "becoming increasingly diverse ethnically and racially - a challenge to all public services including libraries."

This project builds on tools developed for Partnerships for Change and training developed for CORE all of which help staff improve service to all the people in the community, as well as the present library users.

It also provides a new tool, the staff training manual which increases staff proficiency in practical and behavioral techniques for improving communication with multicultural, multiethnic and multilingual populations.

16. Evaluation process.

The evaluation process is incorporated into the project components. The manual will be evaluated by the trainers as they use it and by the participants after the training is completed. The training will be evaluated to determine its strengths and weaknesses. Staff from the participating libraries will meet in focus groups at the project's conclusion to evaluate the experience. ETI, the evaluators for Partnership for Change will be asked to develop the basic design and instruments for testing this project based on their three year experience with PFC. An appropriate instrument should be developed during the project for use at least nine months later.

The concept of working with community consultants is new for libraries not engaged in Partnerships for Change. This project will provide a means for testing the most effective use of this community resource. Throughout the project the director will work closely with the consultants to identify techniques that work and problems that need to be solved. ETI should also be helpful with this element of the evaluation.

If the project continues for a second year, more librarians throughout the State can be trained and more information on the program's effectiveness can be collected.

17. Methods of Continuation:

A second year of this project would allow for an appropriate length of time to complete some critical tests including:

. reviewing the manual in detail and editing or adding to it after a year of experience using it.
. evaluating the effectiveness of the training after a year's experience.
. training staff in other libraries in the State to use the techniques developed in this project.
. providing additional training to staff trained in the first year so they could develop skill as trainers.

The training of trainers is not a new model in the State and builds on the CORE model.

Another tool that could designed in the second year is a training video. The growth in the usage of the training videos in the PLS training center indicates that this format could be used to begin or enhance training in practical skills for working with diverse populations.

Given enough time the training and manual designed for this project will develop skills that are integrated into the service philosophy and behavior of the participants. The motivation of public service staff in the participating libraries to provide the diverse elements in their communities with best possible service increases the value of this project and insures its continuation. A three ring binder makes the manual readily transportable and allows other libraries to use and modify it.

Project Title Staff Training for a Multicultural Environment

Applicant Jurisdiction Peninsula Library System

18. Program budget: LSCA funds requested.

	Advisory Committee (1)	Community Consultants (2)	Develop Manual (3)	Train public service staff (4)	test skills (5)	Evaluate training (6)	TOTAL (7)
a. Salaries: list personnel Project Director FT	6,850	10,572	14,516			5,100	37,038
Benefits	1,600	1,800	2,000			1,272	6,672
@ ___ %							
SUBTOTAL	8,450	12,372	16,516			6,372	43,710
b. Library Materials	0	0	0	500	0	0	500
c. Operation:							
Telecom							
Travel	350	200	300	100	500	1,000	2,450
Supplies	50		700				750
Postage	0	150					150
Printing			2,500				2,500
Contractual	0	14,400	4,000	15,000	2,000	9,000	44,400
SUBTOTAL	400	14,750	7,500	15,100	2,500	10,000	50,250

Project Title Staff Training for a Multicultural Environment

Applicant Jurisdiction Peninsula Library System

18. Program budget: LSCA funds requested.

	Advisory Committee (1)	Community Consultants (2)	Develop resource curriculum (3)	Train public service staff (4)	test skills (5)	evaluate training (6)	TOTAL (7)
d. Equipment over $5,000							
e. Indirect cost 10%	xxx	xxx	xxx	xxx	xxx	xxx	9,446
f. TOTAL LSCA	8,850	27,122	24,016	15,600	2,500	16,372	9,446
						TOTAL	103,906
g. Other funds							0
h. In-Kind	6,000	1,180	2,080	20,380	1,180	1,180	32,000
TOTAL PROJECT	14,850	28,302	26,096	35,980	3,680	17,552	135,906

19. Narrative support for budget.

Salaries and benefits:
Full-time project director at Librarian II, Step II level

Travel includes:

. mileage for project director, resource consultant(s) and
community consultant to meetings and training in San Mateo
and Santa Clara Counties

. air fare and expenses for evaluator(s) based in Los Angeles
five trips to the bay area $150 per trip = $750

Contractual includes:

. resource consultant(s) 12 days at $1500/day = $18,000
. community consultants 20 days at $120/day = $2,400
  six community consultants x $2400 = $14,400
. evaluation of project $12,000
  115 hours at $100/hr = $11,500 plus $500 for report = $12,000

The indirect cost will be used toward use of space and utilities
at PLS administrative headquarters and assistance from PLS clerical,
and financial staff. It also includes the time of the PLS director
and business manager to administer the project.

In-kind:

Salary
  Advisory Committee
  6 librarians $25/hr X 40 hours = $ 6,000

  Staff training in six libraries
  $15/hr X 80 hours staff = $1200
  $1200 x 20 hours = $24,000

                    Sub-total $30,000

Operating Expense
  Library space for training
  and meetings $100/day x 20 days $ 2,000

                    TOTAL $32,000 .

Project Title _____

Applicant Jurisdiction _____ . _____

20. Certification.

   a. I affirm that the jurisdiction or agency named below is the legally designated fiscal agent for this program and is authorized to receive and expend funds for the conduct of this program.

   b. I affirm that any or all other agencies participating in the program have agreed to the terms of the application/grant award, and have entered into an agreement(s) concerning the final disposition of equipment, facilities, and materials purchased for this program from the funds awarded for the activities and services described in the attached, as approved and/or as amended application.

(Signed) _____
                 Authorized representative   Date

(Printed) _____
                 Name and title

Organization _____

Street/mail address _____

City _____ County _____ ZIP+4 _____

Telephone _____ FAX _____

Attachment 1

ADVISORY COMMITTEE

Daly City
Lolly Pineda, Reference Librarian

East Palo Alto
Teri Titus, Acting Branch Librarian

Redwood City
Valentin Porras, Branch Supervisor

Santa Clara, Milpitas Community Library
Linda Arbaugh

Santa Clara Public Library
Anne Sklenskey, Reference Supervisor

Sunnyvale
Marian Hartshorn

Project Title Staff Training for a Multicultural Environment

APPENDIX C:

DIRECTORY OF STATE HUMANITIES COUNCILS

 FEDERATION OF
STATE HUMANITIES
COUNCILS

REVISED AS OF APR. 2, 1992
Please discard others

DIRECTORY OF STATE HUMANITIES COUNCILS
Spring 1992

Alabama Humanities Foundation
2217 Tenth Court South
Birmingham, AL 35205
Tel: 205/930-0540
Fax: 205/930-0986
Chair: Parham Williams
Ex. Dir.: Robert Stewart

Alaska Humanities Forum
430 West 7th Avenue, Suite 1
Anchorage, AK 99501
Tel: 907/272-5341
Chair: Gerald Wilson
Ex. Dir.: Stephen E. Lindbeck

Arizona Humanities Council
Ellis-Shackelford House
1242 North Central Avenue
Phoenix, AZ 85004
Tel: 602/257-0335
Fax: 602/257-0392
Chair: A. Thomas Cole
Ex. Dir.: Dan Shilling

Arkansas Humanities Council
10816 Executive Center Drive
Suite 310
Little Rock, AR 72211
Tel: 501/221-0091
Fax: 501/221-0093
Chair: Mary Toney
Ex. Dir.: Robert Bailey

California Council for the Humanities
312 Sutter, Suite 601
San Francisco, CA 94108
Tel: 415/391-1474
Fax: 415/956-7441
Chair: Don Schweitzer
Ex. Dir.: James Quay

315 West 9th Street, Suite 1103
Los Angeles, CA 90015
Tel: 213/623-5993
Assoc. Dir.: Susan Gordon

**Colorado Endowment for
the Humanities**
1623 Blake Street, Suite 200
Denver, CO 80202
Tel: 303/573-7733
Fax: 303/573-7722
Chair: Donna R. Jones
Ex. Dir.: James Pierce

Connecticut Humanities Council
41 Lawn Avenue
Wesleyan Station
Middletown, CT 06457
Tel: 203/347-6888 or 347-3788
Fax: 203/344-7957
Chair: Michael Helfgott
Ex. Dir.: Bruce Fraser

Delaware Humanities Forum
2600 Pennsylvania Avenue
Wilmington, DE 19806
Tel: 302/573-4410
Fax: 302/573-4424
Chair: Phyllis Levitt
Ex. Dir.: Henry Hirschbiel

D.C. Community Humanities Council
1331 H Street, NW, Suite 902
Washington, DC 20005
Tel: 202/347-1732
Fax: 202/347-3350
Chair: Olivia Cadaval
Ex. Dir.: Francine C. Cary

Florida Humanities Council
1514 1/2 East Eighth Avenue
Tampa, FL 33605-3708
Tel: 813/272-3473
Fax: 813/248-1375
Chair: Carl C. Andersen
Ex. Dir.: Ann Henderson

Georgia Humanities Council
1556 Clifton Road, NE
Emory University
Atlanta, GA 30322
Tel: 404/727-7500
Fax: 404/727-0206
Chair: Alexa Henderson
Ex. Dir.: Ronald Benson

Guam Humanities Council
123 Archbishop Flores Street
Suite C
Agana, Guam 96910
Tel: 671/472-4507
Fax: 671/472-4524
Chair: George J. Boughton
Ex. Dir.: Kathleen Roos

Hawaii Committee for the Humanities
First Hawaiian Bank Building
3599 Waialae Avenue, Room 23
Honolulu, HI 96816
Tel: 808/732-5402
Chair: Esther Kwon Arinaga
Ex. Dir.: Annette Lew

Idaho Humanities Council
217 West State Street
Boise, ID 83702
Tel: 208/345-5346
Fax: 208/345-5347
Chair: Vincent Hannity
Pres.: Thomas McClanahan

Illinois Humanities Council
618 South Michigan
Chicago, IL 60605
Tel: 312/939-5212
Fax: 312/939-1265
Chair: Maynard Wishner
Ex. Dir.: Frank Pettis

Indiana Humanities Council
1500 North Delaware Street
Indianapolis, IN 46202
Tel: 317/638-1500
Fax: 317/634-9503
Chair: P. Donald Herring
Pres.: Kenneth Gladish

Iowa Humanities Board
Oakdale Campus
University of Iowa
Iowa City, IA 52242
Tel: 319/335-4153
Fax: 319/335-4077
Chair: Wayne Moyer
Ex. Dir.: Rick Knupfer

Kansas Committee for the Humanities
112 West Sixth Street
Suite 210
Topeka, KS 66603
Tel: 913/357-0359
Chair: Charlotte Rohrbach
Ex. Dir.: Marion Cott

Kentucky Humanities Council
417 Clifton Avenue
University of Kentucky
Lexington, KY 40508-3406
Tel: 606/257-5932
Chair: M. Janice Murphy
Ex. Dir.: Virginia Smith

**Louisiana Endowment for
the Humanities**
The Ten-O-One Building
1001 Howard Avenue, Suite 3110
New Orleans, LA 70113
Tel: 504/523-4352
Fax: 504/529-2358
Chair: A. David Barry
Pres.: Michael Sartisky

Maine Humanities Council
P.O. Box 7202
Portland, ME 04112
Tel: 207/773-5051
Fax: 207/773-2416
Chair: Tom Tracy
Ex. Dir.: Dorothy Schwartz

Maryland Humanities Council
516 N. Charles St., Suite 201
Baltimore, MD 21201
Tel: 410/625-4830
Fax: 410/625-4834
Chair: Freeman A. Hrabowski III
Ex. Dir.: Naomi Collins

**Massachusetts Foundation for
the Humanities**
One Woodbridge Street
South Hadley, MA 01075
Tel: 413/536-1385
Fax: 413/534-6918
Chair: Joyce Antler
Ex. Dir.: David Tebaldi

80 Boylston Street
Suite 1000
Boston, MA 02116
Tel: 617/451-9021
Assoc. Dir.: Gail Reimer

Michigan Humanities Council
119 Pere Marquette Drive, Suite 3B
Lansing, MI 48912-1231
Tel: 517/372-7770
Fax: 517/372-0027
Chair: Marilyn L. Williamson
Ex. Dir.: Ronald Means

5201 Woodward Avenue, Fourth Floor
Detroit, MI 48202-4093
Tel: 313/993-7770
Prog. Ofc.: Lori S. Naples-Poirier

Minnesota Humanities Commission
26 East Exchange Street
St. Paul, MN 55101
Tel: 612/224-5739
Fax: 612/224-0419
Chair: Burton M. Nygren
Pres.: Cheryl Dickson

Mississippi Humanities Council
3825 Ridgewood Road, Room 508
Jackson, MS 39211
Tel: 601/982-6752
Chair: Thomas W. Lewis, III
Ex. Dir.: Cora Norman

Missouri Humanities Council
911 Washington Avenue, Suite 215
St. Louis, MO 63101-1208
Tel: 314/621-7705
Fax: 314/621-5850
Chair: Jane Frick
Ex. Dir.: Christine J. Reilly

**Montana Committee for
the Humanities**
P.O. Box 8036
Hellgate Station
Missoula, MT 59807
Tel: 406/243-6022
Fax: 406/243-2748
Chair: Walter Fleming
Ex. Dir.: Margaret Kingsland

Nebraska Humanities Council
Lincoln Ctr. Bldg., #225
215 Centennial Mall South
Lincoln, NE 68508
Tel: 402/474-2131
Fax: 402/474-4852
Chair: Darrel Lloyd
Ex. Dir.: Jane R. Hood

Nevada Humanities Committee
P.O. Box 8029
1101 N. Virginia Street
Reno, NV 89507
Tel: 702/784-6587
Fax: 702/784-1300
Chair: Mary-Ellen McMullen
Ex. Dir.: Judith Winzeler

Southern Office
4765 Brussels Avenue
Las Vegas, NV 89119
Tel: 702/798-0337
Asst. Dir.: Joseph Finkhouse

New Hampshire Humanities Council
19 Pillsbury Street
P.O. Box 2228
Concord, NH 03301-2228
Tel: 603/224-4071
Fax: 603/224-4072
Chair: Anne C. Zachos
Ex. Dir.: Charles Bickford

**New Jersey Committee for
the Humanities**
73 Easton Avenue
New Brunswick, NJ 08901
Tel: 908/932-7726
Fax: 908/932-1179
Chair: Walter T. Savage
Ex. Dir.: Miriam L. Murphy

**New Mexico Endowment for
the Humanities**
209 Onate Hall
Corner of Campus & Girard NE
Albuquerque, NM 87131
Tel: 505/277-3705
Chair: Juanita Palmerhall
Ex. Dir.: John Lucas

New York Council for the Humanities
198 Broadway, 10th Floor
New York, NY 10038
Tel: 212/233-1131
Fax: 212/233-4607
Chair: Geoffrey G. Field
Ex. Dir.: Jay Kaplan

North Carolina Humanities Council
425 Spring Garden Street
Greensboro, NC 27401
Tel: 919/334-5325
Chair: Robert F. Yeager
Ex. Dir.: Alice Barkley

North Dakota Humanities Council
P.O. Box 2191
Bismarck, ND 58502
Tel: 701/255-3360
Fax: 701/223-8724
Chair: Donald Wharton
Ex. Dir.: Everett Albers

Ohio Humanities Council
695 Bryden Road
P.O. Box 06354
Columbus, OH 43206-0354
Tel: 614/461-7802
Fax: 614/461-4651
Chair: John Gabel
Ex. Dir.: Eleanor Wilkie Kingsbury

**Oklahoma Foundation for
the Humanities**
Festival Plaza
428 West California, Suite 270
Oklahoma City, OK 73102
Tel: 405/235-0280
Fax: 405/235-0289
Chair: Nancy Phillips
Ex. Dir.: Anita May

Oregon Council for the Humanities
812 SW Washington, Suite 225
Portland, OR 97205
Tel: 503/241-0543
Fax: 503/241-0024
Chair: Arnold Biskar
Ex. Dir.: Richard Lewis

Pennsylvania Humanities Council
320 Walnut Street, #305
Philadelphia, PA 19106
Tel: 215/925-1005
Fax: 215/925-3054
Chair: Christopher N. Breiseth
Ex. Dir.: Craig Eisendrath

**Fundacion Puertorriquena de
las Humanidades**
Apartado Postal S-4307
San Juan de Puerto Rico 00904
Tel: 809/721-2087
Fax: 809/722-2130
Chair: Hiram R. Cancio
Ex. Dir.: Juan M. Gonzalez Lamela

Bacon House Mews
606 18th Street, NW, 2nd Floor
Washington, D.C. 20006
Tel: 202/371-8111
Coor: Paquita Vivo

**Rhode Island Committee for
the Humanities**
60 Ship Street
Providence, RI 02903
Tel: 401/273-2250
Fax: 401/454-4872
Chair: Judith Swift
Ex. Dir.: Thomas Roberts

South Carolina Humanities Council
1610 Oak Street
Columbia, SC 29204
Tel: 803/771-8864
Chair: Elaine Freeman
Ex. Dir.: Randy Akers

South Dakota Humanities Council
Box 7050, University Station
Brookings, SD 57007
Tel: 605/688-6113
Chair: Cathryn Spelts
Ex. Dir.: John Whalen

Tennessee Humanities Council
P.O. Box 24767
Nashville, TN 37202
Tel: 615/320-7001
Fax: 615/321-4586
Chair: G. Cecil Woods
Ex. Dir.: Robert Cheatham

Texas Committee for the Humanities
3809 S. Second Street
Austin, TX 78704
Tel: 512/440-1991
Fax: 512/440-0115
Chair: Everett L. Fly
Ex. Dir.: James Veninga

Utah Humanities Council
Ten West Broadway, Suite 505
Salt Lake City, UT 84101
Tel: 801/531-7868
Fax: 801/531-7869
Chair: F. Ross Peterson
Ex. Dir.: Delmont Oswald

Vermont Council on the Humanities
P.O. Box 58
Hyde Park, VT 05655
Tel: 802/888-3183
Fax: 802/888-7212
Chair: Mary Ann Chaffee
Ex. Dir.: Victor Swenson

**Virginia Foundation for
the Humanities**
145 Ednam Drive
Charlottesville, VA 22903
Tel: 804/924-3296
Fax: 804/296-4714
Chair: Rosel Schewel
Pres.: Robert Vaughan

Virgin Islands Humanities Council
P.O. Box 1829
St. Thomas, VI 00803
Tel: 809/776-4044
Fax: 809/779-8294
Chair: Vincent O. Cooper
Ex. Dir.: Magda Smith

**Washington Commission for
the Humanities**
615 Second Avenue, Suite 300
Seattle, WA 98104
Tel: 206/682-1770
Fax: 206/682-4158
Chair: Delma Tayer
Ex. Dir.: Hidde Van Duym

West Virginia Humanities Council
723 Kanawha Blvd., Suite 800
Charleston, WV 25301
Tel: 304/346-8500
Fax: 304/346-8504
Chair: Alan B. Gould
Ex. Dir.: Charles Daugherty

Wisconsin Humanities Committee
716 Langdon Street
Madison, WI 53706
Tel: 608/262-0706
Chair: Carol Tennessen
Ex. Dir.: Patricia Anderson

**Wyoming Council for the
Humanities**
Box 3643, University Station
Laramie, WY 82071-3643
Tel: 307/766-6496
Chair: Maggi Murdock
Ex. Dir.: Robert G. Young

APPENDIX D:

ALA *POETS IN PERSON* APPLICATION FORM

POETS IN PERSON

**Demonstration Project
Library Application**

"Poets in Person": Reading, Hearing, and Talking About Contemporary Poetry in America's Libraries

What is "Poets in Person"?

"Poets in Person": Reading, Hearing, and Talking About Contemporary Poetry in America's Libraries, a project of the Modern Poetry Association (publishers of *Poetry* Magazine), the American Library Association, and the National Endowment for the Humanities, is designed to promote and support humanities programming — poetry programming in particular — in public libraries.

Through a simple application process, 20 libraries around the country will be selected to participate. Each library will offer a 5- to 10-week series of weekly poetry discussion programs led by a local humanities scholar and featuring the new audio series "Poets in Person," produced by the Modern Poetry Association and premiering on National Public Radio this summer.

What will the 20 participating libraries receive?

■ The opportunity to send a team of three people—a library staff person, a local scholar, and a representative of a state support group—to a national training seminar and workshop to be held November 7-9, 1991. All seminar expenses, including travel and meals, will be covered by the project.

■ A budget to pay honoraria for local scholars.

■ Complete sets of audiocassettes for the 14-part "Poets in Person" series.

■ Support print materials: a Listener's Guide to the series, giving concise critical and biographical information, annotated reading lists, and texts of the poems for each poet in the series; a Programmer's Guide with step-by-step assistance in planning and carrying out the programs; and a publicity kit to promote the series.

■ A budget to expand the library's modern poetry collection.

■ An exciting new library program.

What will be expected of participating libraries?

■ A meeting place, either at the library or in the community.

■ Staff time to plan, promote, and put on the series.

■ Recruitment of one team member for the seminar from either the state library, state library association, or state humanities council.

■ Endorsement by the library's administration and board, by signature on this application form.

■ A short written evaluation at the conclusion of the project.

■ Enthusiasm about offering a new poetry program in libraries.

What will be expected of the participating state agency?

■ Endorsement of the library's participation (signature on application form) and willingness to assist through donated time and/or services.

■ Agreement to share their project experience with other librarians in the state.

What will the selection committee be looking for in choosing the 20 demonstration sites?

■ A regional geographic mix.

■ A mixture of urban, suburban, and rural libraries.

■ Libraries that are new to reading and discussion programming.

■ Targeted audiences.

■ Strong support from a state agency or association, the library's administration and the community. (A letter of support from any of these groups is encouraged.)

Please note: Not being able to name a local scholar at the time of this application will not eliminate a library from consideration. State humanities agencies will be able to help find qualified and interested scholars.

Final selection of the 20 participating libraries will be made by the "Poets in Person" Project Advisory Board.

Poets featured in the 14 half-hour "Poets in Person" audio programs are:

A. R. Ammons
John Ashbery
Gwendolyn Brooks
Rita Dove
Allen Ginsberg
Maxine Kumin
W.S. Merwin
James Merrill
Sharon Olds
Adrienne Rich
Karl Shapiro
Gary Soto
Charles Wright
A special "Introduction to Poets in Person" program gives an overview of the series

Please complete the attached application form and return it by **September 6, 1991,** to:

"Poets in Person" Project Applications
Modern Poetry Association
60 West Walton Street
Chicago, IL 60610

If you have any questions or require help in completing the application, please call the Project office: 312-280-4870.

POETS IN PERSON

"Poets in Person" Project
Application Form

Name of Library

Address

City   State   ZIP

Phone

Name/title of person to be in charge of "Poets in Person" Project

Tell us about your library (size and makeup of the community, special populations served, library community activities, etc.):

What is your target audience for this program? Why?

What experience has your library had with presenting humanities programming (e.g., participation in the "Let's Talk About It" project)?

_____

_____

_____

_____

_____

Are you currently participating in the NEH-ALA "Voices & Visions" pilot project?

_____

What kinds of support can you draw on for this program (state library, state humanities council, local scholars, friends of the library, local poetry or writing group, etc.)? You are encouraged to send a letter of support from any of these groups with your application.

_____

_____

_____

In what ways will they provide assistance?

_____

_____

_____

_____

We hereby apply to be a demonstration library for the project "Poets in Person": Reading, Hearing, and Talking About Contemporary Poetry in America's Libraries. We agree to provide staff time and a meeting location for a 5- to 10-week program series, as well as support in promotion of the series.

_____

Library Director

We hereby endorse the application of the library named above and agree to support their participation through donated time and/or services.

_____

State Agency Representative
(state library, state humanities council, or state library association)

APPENDIX E:

MERCED COUNTY LIBRARY GRANT APPLICATION: "COLUMBUS AND AFTER..."

MERCED COUNTY LIBRARY
2100 "O" STREET
TELEPHONE (AREA CODE 209) 385-7484
MERCED, CALIFORNIA 95340
FAX NUMBER (209) 726-7912

January 17, 1992

Dr. Jim Quay, Director
California Council for the Humanities
312 Sutter Street, Suite 601
San Francisco, CA 94108

Dear Dr. Quay:

The Merced County Library would like to submit our
application for a minigrant entitled "Columbus and After:
Rethinking the Legacy." Enclosed is our application,
including a brief description of our vision of how the
program would be held, a budget, and the vita of Mr.
Cardoza, our scholar.

Humanities programming is well received in our public
library. The three book groups we have held recently have
been well received by our patrons. We know this new one
would be as successful.

Sincerely,

Linda Wilson
County Librarian

Dee Near
Technical Services Librarian

enc.

LW/kc

COLUMBUS AND AFTER : READING AND DISCUSSION GROUP

Merced is proud to be a site for of the "Columbus and After : Rethinking the Legacy" Chautauqua this coming July. The local sponsors are working together to make this a total community event. An interest in the themes that the chautauqua will explore is already evident in the area. Many small donations have been made by private citizens in an effort to make our local budget, and service groups in Merced are volunteering to help with the details during the week.

We feel that a reading and discussion series prior to the coming of the chautauqua would give participants an opportunity to pursue the theme of the initial and ongoing cultural encounter between persons involved with the history of our country. The Merced County Library would like to be the sponsor and site of the reading and discussion programs centering on the theme "Columbus and After : Rethinking the Legacy." Mr. Art Cardoza, Professor of History at Merced College, would be the scholar leading the group. Mr. Cardoza successfully moderated our "Trails" book reading and discussion sessions in the Spring of 1991.

I. WHERE AND WHEN: Discussions would be held Thursday
evenings from 7- 9 pm in the Gracey Room of the Merced
County Library. The dates would be April 30, May 7 and 21
and June 4, 1992. Evening meetings are planned in order to
include the working adult.

II. PUBLICITY: Publicity would be distributed through local
service organizations, established news media, and through
the library. The newspaper, the Merced Sun Star, does a
regular feature on the library in the "Living " Section.
The newsletters of the local organizations, such as American
Association of University Women and the League of Women
Voters, would include announcements. The Regional Arts
Council newsletter would also advertise the programs.
Flyers designed by the library would be posted at grocery
stores and local shops in the communities of Merced and
Atwater as well as in the nineteen libraries in our county.

There is a core of persons interested in such programs.
The Merced County Library has sponsored discussion groups in
the past two years, and all have been very popular.
We have had an average attendance of between 18 and 20
persons at our book groups held here in Merced. Themes
included "The Common Good," "Trails" and "Vietnam." There
was a little duplication of attendance, but we drew from many
segements of our population with each theme. A

reservation list would be made available for people to sign up during late February and March once the publicity is released.

III. READINGS

The Reader which is being compiled to accompany the Chautauqua event would be the source of readings for the participants. The Reader will include pieces by each Chautauquan on their characters, excerpts from writings on other cultural encounters and will provide additional perspectives on the idea of "cultural encounters" in the western world. The book reading and discussion series will allow for the public to anticipate the Chautauqua with a greater knowledge of the issues at hand.

```
          BUDGET FOR "COLUMBUS" READING DISCUSSION GROUP
                      MERCED COUNTY LIBRARY


Scholar honoraria. 4 sessions @ $150 each      $600.00

Flyers advertising the program                   20.00
  200 at $.10 per sheet


Reader photocopies. Copies for                  300.00
  scholar and participants                     _____
  of reader prepared to accompany
  Chautauqua. $10 per x 30

                        TOTAL      $      920.00
```

VITA

Arthur J. Cardoza

2434 Brookdale Court
Merced, California 95340
(209) 722-6422

Education: M.A. Degree, Social Science, 1973, California State University,
             Sacramento
             B.A. Degree, Social Science, 1972, California State University,
             Sacramento
             Credentials from State of California
                 Administrative Services
                 Pupil Personnel Services
                 Community College Instructor
                 Standard Secondary

Experience: College Instructor, Merced College, 1980 to present.
             Courses taught in all social science areas to include U.S.
             History, History of the Southwest, Introduction to Social Science,
             Introduction to Psychology, and Introduction to Sociology.

             Instructor and Counselor, Fresno City College , Fresno, Calif.
             summers of 1979, 1979 and 1980

             Instructor of Sociology, College of the Sequoias, Visalia, Calif.
             evening college, 1975-80

             Lecturer, CSU Bakersfield, 1979, Office of Extended Education

             Counselor, Mt. Whitney High School. Visalia Calif. 1975-80

             Coordinator EOP & S Program, American River College, Sacramento,
             Calif.

Related
Experience: Scholar, California Council for the Humanities. Reading and dis-
                 cussion group leader on the theme "Trails: Toward a New
                 Western History. Merced County Library, Spring, 1991
             Guest Lecture, Cultural Unity Forum, 1989, Merced College
             Presenter, Migrant Education Workshop, 1988, CSU Stanislaus
             Guest Lecture, Social Science Speaker Circuit 1986, Merced College
             President, Merced College Faculty Senate 1986
             Grant Proposal Writer, College of the Sequoias, 1976

Community
Activities: Trustee, Merced City School District 1989
             President, Merced Kiwanis Club, 1987-88
             Chairman of Merced City Planning Commission, 1986
             Merced City Planning Commission, 1981-87
             President, Mexican American Golf Association, 1985-86
             President, Mexican American Educators Association, 1977

Hobbies: Golf, baseball, boating, tennis

References: Available upon request

APPENDIX F:

MARSHALL PUBLIC LIBRARY GRANT APPLICATIONS AND LETTERS OF SUPPORT

PROPOSAL FOR EZRA JACK KEATS MINI-GRANT OF $500

Because we believe literacy and the love of reading begins at an early age with listening, we propose to offer a program for parents and their children 3 to 6 years of age, and their teachers, to emphasize the importance of this skill. We will present a three day listening series with a storyteller/puppeteer called: "THE LISTENING FESTIVAL AT THE LIBRARY" in celebration of the Marshall Public Library's first birthday.

Day 1: Half hour session of "Stories with Puppets" with a storyteller/puppeteer in the morning and repeated in the afternoon. Parents and their children, and teachers are invited to attend together and will hear stories based on children's picture books which will be available in the library. After each session the storyteller will explain the power of using puppets as a listening tool and will share patterns for simple puppets with parents and teachers. While the storyteller is with the adults (about 1/2 hour), the children will be with a caregiver(s) and have picture books to look at and puppets to explore.

Day 2: Half hour session of "Stories with Picture Books" in the morning, repeated in the afternoon. Visual aids, such as flannelboards, will be used in addition to books. With the adults, the storyteller will emphasize how to choose books for reading aloud and how to feel at ease with books and young children. The session will be structured the same as above, with a variety of easy visual aid patterns to share.

Day 3: Half hour session of "Stories: from Me to You" (traditional storytelling without aids) in the morning, repeated in the afternoon. All stories will be selected from quality children's literature. Afterwards the storyteller will give confidence boosting tips and exercises to encourage parents and teachers to try storytelling too. Session will be structured as before.

```
BUDGET: Storyteller/puppeteer...................................$390.00
        Books to supplement collection..........................  65.00
        Child care to augment volunteered services
            (These funds applied to books if enough volunteers
             can be recruited to provide the child care).......  25.00
        Publicity - fliers and postage
            (Sent to schools, churches and posted locally)......  20.00

                                          TOTAL................ $500.00
```

EZRA JACK KEATS FOUNDATION
1005 East 4th Street
Brooklyn, NY 11230
(718) 252-4047

A P P L I C A T I O N   F O R $ 5 0 0   M I N I - G R A N T
(To be postmarked <u>no later</u> than September 15, 1991)

Date of Application September 10, 1991

Name of Organization Marshall Public Library

1) Briefly describe the location of your library and the number, type and age of the population you serve.

Marshall, Missouri, is the county seat of Saline County. It is a small rural community, population 12,781, in the center of the state. A liberal arts institution, Missouri Valley College with an enrollment of 1300, is located here. The library serves a diverse population - pre-school and school age children; college students, both local and commuters; adults working on their GED; developmentally disabled clients living at the Habilitation Center; disabled senior citizens in group homes; business people and those looking for jobs; and adults who enjoy leisure reading.

2) Describe the program for which you seek funding.

The library is offering a program series during 1991 and 92 called "Newbery Celebration: The Best of the Best." It will be a nine month celebration culminating with a special program for parents and children in observance of the second anniversary of the Marshall Public Library. Children will participate in the library for at least two hours each week. A different Newbery award winner will be highlighted each month. Activities each week will be interdisciplinary and structured to include a game, a craft, food, and information. The Ezra Jack Keats Foundation grant would be used to bring a Newbery award-winning author to Marshall for the special program during our anniversary week. This author visit and program in the library would highlight the "Newbery Celebration".

3) How many people do you expect to serve with this program? at least 300 children, parents, and teachers.

4) Include a budget breakdown for the project, demonstrating how these monies will be used.

Budget Item	Library	Foundation
Children's leader 72 hrs. with children 216 hrs. preparation @$5/hr.	$1440	
Materials including publicity fliers, etc.	$540	
Newbery paperbacks for each child participating	$900	
Author honorarium and expenses		$500

5) Have you received a Mini-Grant from this foundation in the past?

   X YES In what years?   1990

   ____NO

PLEASE NOTE: $500 Mini-Grants from the Ezra Jack Keats Foundation are to be used to instill a love of literature in children, and to foster literacy and creativity. Programs that will be considered include storytelling, innovative or noteworthy workshops, lectures, and festivals, as well as programs targeted at parents. Funds are not to be used primarily for the purchase of books and tapes, for general operations, administrative costs, transportation of the audience, and the like. Decisions will be announced by mail in December 1991.

ONLY ONE APPLICATION WILL BE CONSIDERED FROM EACH LIBRARY.

APPLICATION FORM

1. Library Marshall Public Library   Date March 15, 1991

     Address 214 North Lafayette B   Phone (816) 886-3391

      Marshall, MO 65340   LSCA Title I

2. Population: Library District 12781   Served by Project 1303

3. Project Target Area County   4. LSCA Category #2 Inadequately Serv.

5. Brief description of project:

This project will provide a business information center for small businesses, non-profits, job-seekers, and those desiring a career change.

6. How does this project relate to Missouri's Long-Range Program for Library Service?

This project relates to Goal II "assist local libraries to increase services and/or improve the quality of existing services in areas where populations are inadequately served."

7.
PROJECT BUDGET	LSCA Funds Requested	State Funds* to be used	Local Funds* to be used	Total Funds
Salaries/Wages (inc. fringe)				
Books	$19,222			$19,222
Audiovisual Materials				
Equipment (including AV)	664			664
Contract Services				
Other				
TOTAL	$19,886			$19,886

*These must be documented in the same manner as federal funds.

8. Library Information:
    Number hours open per week 69
    Library income $145,090
    Number of staff (FTE) 2.9
    Amount paid in salaries $53,728
    Materials expenditures $53,175
    Total expenditures $145,090
    Total volumes owned 15,661
    Total circulation 4024/mo

This project has been approved by the library board of trustees:

_X_ ~~President, Board of Trustees~~   2/26/91
President, Board of Trustees   Date

Wicky Slight   2/25/91
Library Director   Date

9. LSCA Advisory Committee $_____

10. Approved for funding $_____

L-1-001-R2 (MoSL)   Project No. _____

Marshall Public Library
LSCA Application Form
March 15, 1991
Economic Development

Section I. Background Information

The Marshall Public Library opened on March 19, 1990. Since
then, the Library has grown to over 15,000 volumes.
Interlibrary loan and data base searching are used by
patrons on a daily basis. Fiscal year 1991 LSCA grants have
enabled the Library to provide over 1000 titles for adult
new readers, a basic reference collection and non-fiction
books for children in grades 5 through 8, and hardware which
makes interlibrary loan possible. Circulation averages
almost 4000 volumes per month.

According to the 1989 Social and Economic Profile, published
by the University of Missouri Extension office, there are
523 small businesses (under 20 employees) in Saline County.
There are approximately 12 non-profit organizations which
employ from 1 to 100.

The Library acts as a partner with the Marshall Chamber of
Commerce, the Marshall-Saline Development Corporation and
local businesses to promote business retention and economic
development. The five local accounting firms each donated
funds to allow the library to purchase a set of state
personal income tax forms from Commerce Clearing House.
Another local businessman provided funds for a set of
telephone directories for all Missouri cities and towns on
microfiche.

Section II. Statement of User or Community Need.

Saline County is on the southern border of the seriously
declining northern tier of Missouri counties. Its
population declined by 15 percent from 1940 to 1980, and has
continued to decline by 2% from 1980 to 1987. Compared to
the state distribution, Saline County has a greater
proportion of households with effective buying incomes
(after taxes) below $20,000 - an estimated 57% compared to
42% statewide in 1987. (Missouri University. Extension,
Social and Economic Profile, 1989, Saline County).

Marshall Public Library
LSCA Application Form
March 15, 1991
Economic Development

The total of residential permits issued for 1990 (4) in
Marshall was the lowest in a decade. In 1980 there were 102
housing starts.

The 1990 Wage Rates in Selected Occupations for Carroll and
Saline Counties (Missouri Division of Employment Security,
November, 1990) states that "Since the area's economy
depends largely on that of the farming sector, the hardships
experienced by agriculture in recent years have taken their
toll. Some employers in the area have made some serious
staffing cutbacks in recent years. One major manufacturer
has cut its staff to a very small fraction of its original
size and other large manufacturers have closed their doors.

"Health care providers and hospitals have also seen some
reductions in staffing. Because of the advent of outpatient
surgical procedures and the improved health of the
population, this trend will probably continue".

The second largest employer, Wilson Foods, virtually closed
its plant in August when its workforce went from 750 to 80.
This alone has had a severe impact on the economy. In
Demcember, 1990, there were 768 persons unemployed in Saline
County.

In The Autobiography of Benjamin Franklin, Franklin stated
that the early subscription libraries, the forerunner of the
modern public library, "made the common tradesman and
farmers as intelligent as most gentlemen from other
countries, and perhaps have contributed in some degree to
the stand so generally made throughout the colonies in
defense of their privileges." The information needs of
today's small businesses become even more vital as they
struggle to maintain economic viability.

The local pizza store owner needs information on
incorporating; the new mother wants to start a home-based
business; the non-profit agency needs information on grants;
the state worker wants career advancement and needs to know
how to write a resume. He also needs a typewriter on which
to type it. The Missouri Career Guide (Missouri
Occupational Information Coordinating Committee, 1990)
promises the worker who was laid off that "the information
you need (to find a job) may be in the library."

Marshall Public Library
LSCA Application Form
March 15, 1991
Economic Development

The cottage industries which have sprung up as a replacement
to agriculture need information on marketing, business
travelling, promoting, and a host of other subjects. The
auto parts store owner needs to find an obscure part. The
small business owner needs to know a zip code and how to
address certain types of business correspondence.

Section III. List Goals and Measurable Objectives.

Goal - To provide essential business information to the 523
small businesses, the 12 non-profit associations, and the
768 unemployed thereby promoting business retention and
encouraging economic development.

Objectives - By June 30, 1992, identify at least two new
jobs which have been created in Marshall through the use of
the library information center and five people who have
found permanent employment.

Section IV. Methods to be used to Accomplish the Goals and
Objectives.

● Select individuals as members of Focus Groups to set
guidelines, determine the kind of information needed, and
define potential audiences.

● Use the following bibliography to select a core
collection based on specific needs of the community as
defined by the Focus Groups:

   -The Basic Business Library: Core Resources. Ed. by
Bernard S. Schlessinger. 2nd ed. Oryx, 1989.

   -Encyclopedia of Business Information Sources. Ed. by
James Way. 8th ed. Gale, 1990.

   -Kennedy, Joyce Lain. Home Businesses Under $5000. Sun
Features, 1989.

   -Kingstone, Brett. The Student Entrepreneur's Guide:
How To Start Your Own Business. Rev. and updated. 1990.

Marshall Public Library
LSCA Application Form
March 15, 1991
Economic Development

-Lavin, Michael R. <u>Business Information: How to Find It, How to Use It</u>. Oryx, 1987.

-<u>Small Business Start-up Index: A Guide to Practical Information Related to Starting a Small Business</u>. Ed. by Michael Madden. Gale, 1990.

-U.S. Small Business Administration. <u>Directory of Business Development Publications.</u> Washington, D.C.: Govt. Print. Off., 1989.

● Utilizing the Focus Groups, plan breakfast programs to introduce the various groups to the business collection.

● Promote use through distributing peel-off telephone labels and preprinted telephone Rolodex cards printed with the Library telephone number.

● Utilize public service announcements, videos, brochures, and posters now being developed by the Public Library Association.

● Provide a special bulletin board for business cards to encourage networking.

● Mount displays highlighting local businesses.

● Provide lunchtime film programs on topics of interest to small business.

● Offer workshops on resume writing and interviewing

● Continue active partnership with the Chamber of Commerce through Librarian serving on committees and attending meetings; the Marshall-Saline Development Corporation; and the local Job Service Employer Committee of which the Librarian is an active member.

Alternative methods of meeting the needs: Continue to provide reference services and interlibrary loan. Utilize Missouri State Library Reference Department and other large metropolitan libraries as resources. Rationale for requested method: These libraries are not set up to function as a business reference resource for other libraries. Additionally, information needs of business and job-seekers are immediate and require immediate answers.

Marshall Public Library
LSCA Application Form
March 15, 1991
Economic Development

Section V. Budget.

ITEM	LSCA FUNDS	LOCAL FUNDS	TOTAL
Books	$19222.00*		$19222
Typewriter	664.00		664

   * Based on the core list of business reference sources
for a small library from The Basic Business Library, 2nd ed.
plus selected titles from bibliographies listed in Section
IV.

Section VI. Methods for Evaluating the Project.

The project will be successful if, by June 30, 1992, the Job
Service Employer Committee and Missouri Division of
Employment Security, together with the Librarian, can
identify two new jobs which have been created and five
people who have found employment through use of the business
information center.

Section VII. Future Plans for the Project.

The project will be continued with local funds. A model
business information center designed for a small library
serving a declining rural population will be established.
The successes, failures, methodology, and bibliographies
will be shared with similar libraries through the library
literature and presentations at library conferences.

Business reference services and use of the collection will
be promoted in the three-county area of Saline, Carroll, and
Chariton. These counties, which do not have county-wide
library service, share a common border and many of the same
economic problems. Librarians in city libraries in these
counties will be invited to become involved in providing
business information through the Marshall Public Library
business center.

FRIENDS OF ARROW ROCK, INC.

Wicky Sleight
Marshall Public Library
Marshall, Missouri

January 25, 1991

Dear Wicky,

I was delighted to hear the Marshall Public Library
is applying for a grant that would provide resources
for small businesses and nonprofit organizations such
as the Friends of Arrow Rock. There is certainly a
need for this specialized information.

While the Friends is a 32 year old historic
preservation organization, we did not have our first
office and full time staff member until 1984. Our
organization has experienced a steady growth and I
feel we provide maximum services for minimum dollars.
In 1990 expenditures of $78,334 provided a full time
staff person, three seasonal tour guides,
administration of children's spring and fall
education programs as well as a regular schedule of
tours of historic buildings in Arrow Rock, and
maintenance of nine historic structures including
major restoration of one of those buildings.

Each year we are allotted only $100 for resource
books. What a wonderful help it would be if we had
access to a number of books that would benefit a wide
range of nonprofit organizations so we could use our
small budget for resources that are more specialized.

For example, it would be such a help if we had access
to resources from the Foundation Center that could be
used for fund raising. Presently I must make a trip
to Kansas City to obtain this needed information.
There are so many good resources on fund raising,
membership, management, editing newsletters, etc.,
all items that would be helpful to a variety of
nonprofits. If these were available for me in
Marshall I could spend my money on specific resources
I need such as" The Cleaning of Masonry Buildings."

The Marshall Library serves a wide area and I know
there are numerous nonprofits such as the Marshall
Philharmonic, Butterfield Youth Services, Mental
Health Association, Missouri Valley College, and
Fitzgibbon Hospital. But I know first hand of the
needs of Arrow Rock.

Arrow Rock, population 82, has three nonprofits: the
Friends, The Historic Arrow Rock Council, and the
Lyceum Theatre. From this community of 82 we serve
82,000 visitors annually. Just think, each
performance of the Lyceum seats over twice the
population of Arrow Rock!

The Arrow Rock Area Merchants Association listed 21
members in 1990. Each one of those businesses is
definitely a small business. Recently our town was
the study project of a group of students from the
University of Missouri who had a class in community
development. After these three young people had
spent some time here talking to the residents and
business people I asked what conclusions they had
reached. One young woman responded, "It seems to me
most people in Arrow Rock hold two jobs, one to keep
Arrow Rock alive, and the other to keep themselves
alive!"

Most of us in Arrow Rock are out there doing our best
to keep it all going. Just think of the benefit that
could be derived from small business information.
What a service this would be to Arrow Rock.

Sincerely,

Kathy Borgman
Executive Director

FLOYD ALSBACH CONSTRUCTION COMPANY

Dear Wicky,

Having started a small business without the benefit of any business experience, I know first hand how dificult business can be. I have survived my first three years through luck, guts, and elbow grease. Now, only now, do I know how much help I needed at the start.

I didn't have anywhere to turn for advice, or explanations, outside of friends and family. I received a great deal of advice, it was mostly conflicting and shallow.

Finally I took a correspondence course on managing a small business. I couldn't believe it, me, after nine years of college and a terminal degree in my field, taking a correspondence course. But... it helped a lot.

I can only imagine how nice it would have been to have had a readily accessable source of information to draw from.

Sincerely,

Floyd Alsbach

P.O. Box 802   Marshall, MO.   65340   816-886-5150

NAPA AUTO PARTS of Marshall

QUALITY AUTOMOTIVE PARTS AND SERVICE

7 E. EASTWOOD ST.
MARSHALL, MISSOURI 65340
816-886-2264

NAPA

February 11, 1991

Mrs. Wicky Sleight
Librarian
Marshall Public Library
214 N. Lafayette
Marshall, MO 65340

Dear Mrs. Sleight:

As a small business owner, I have need for reference material
(sources of supply, conversion factors for foreign parts, etc.) as
well as for help in business management and operations. I have
already made suggestions for library acquisitions which would help
me and hopefully would help others.

Library acquisitions such as I have suggested would reduce the
need for owners to acquire their own business library.

It would certainly be useful to me if the library would
develop a collection on small business operations and management,
as well as general business references such as the Thomas Register.

I also use, and have referred customers to the library for
technical and automotive information.

Sincerely yours,

G. E. Richards
President

**214 North Lafayette B
Marshall, Missouri 65340
(816) 886-3391**

April 29, 1991

Mr. Arthur F. Abelman
Moses & Singer
Time & Life Building
1271 Avenue of the Americas
New York, NY 10020

Dear Mr. Abelman,

Enclosed please find an application from the Marshall
Public Library for a Lois Lenski Covey Foundation grant.

The town of Marshall has discovered the joy of having a
library! During the last year, books and programs have
captured the imagination of the entire community. We want
this excitement to continue as we look forward to the
library's second birthday.

We congratulate the foundation on behalf of libraries
everywhere and look forward to a positive response for this
grant opportunity.

Sincerely,

Wicky Sleight
Library Director

Enclosure

THE LOIS LENSKI COVEY FOUNDATION, INC.

<u>QUESTIONNAIRE</u>

Name and address: Marshall Public Library
214 N. Lafayette B
Marshall, MO 65340

Are you a governmentally-supported school or library?‗yes‗‗‗·

Are you a tax-exempt organization?‗yes‗‗‗·

Are you a private foundation? ‗‗no‗‗‗·

If you are a tax-exempt organization, please enclose a photocopy of the most recent determination letter issued to you by the Internal Revenue Service, and a photocopy of your most recent Annual Report (IRS Form 990).   Federal ID # - 44-6000217

If you are a school, is your school library open to children no longer attending school?‗‗‗‗. What hours?‗‗‗‗·

Please describe the community you serve: See attached

What is your annual budget for the purchase of children's books?‗$21,048 (includes a $15,000 federal grant)

If you are a school, what grades are covered?‗‗‗‗·

how many children are enrolled in your school or use your library regularly?‗circulation is 1516/month

Please describe your library facilities and staff: See attached

How many books do you have in your children's collection?‗2096‗

Are they in good condition?‗‗yes‗‗·

In general, what types of books do you need?Fiction for Grades 3,4,5,
                                                                and 6.

Approximately how many books are needed?‗‗680‗‗‗·

Please estimate the cost of these books‗‗$6900‗‗·

Please give us any additional information you feel would be useful to our directors.   See attached.

How does the per capita income of the area you serve compare to that of your state as a whole?

Our area is: Much higher   ( )

            Higher   ( )

            About the same   ( )

            Lower   (χ)

            Much lower   ( )

Date‗April 29, 1991‗‗   Signed *Wicky Sleight*

LOIS LENSKI COVEY FOUNDATION
GRANT APPLICATION
MARSHALL PUBLIC LIBRARY
Marshall, Mo 65340

Please describe the community you serve:

Marshall, Missouri, the county seat of Saline County, is a
small rural community with a population of 12,781. It is
located 10 miles north of Interstate Highway 35, 80 miles
east of Kansas City, and 185 miles west of St. Louis. A
small liberal arts institution, Missouri Valley College with
an enrollment of 1300, is located here.

Agriculture is a very important part of the economy in
Saline County. In 1989, cash receipts from crops ranked 6th
out of 114 counties in Missouri. The predominant crops are
soybeans, corn, wheat, sorghum and hay. Cattle, hogs and
pigs are the main livestock.

Marshall's economy is strongly tied to agriculture. This
economic base has led to the addition of many industries
associated with the production of farm products. The 1991
Missouri Directory of Manufacturers lists 19 companies in
Marshall. The largest of these is Banquet, ConAgra Frozen
Foods Corporation, which employs 915 people. Most are small
family owned businesses employing under 20.

The population of the county declined by 15 percent from
1940 to 1980, and has continued to decline by 2% from 1980
to 1987. Compared to the state distribution, Saline County
has a greater proportion of households with effective buying
incomes (after taxes) below $20,000 - an estimated 57%
compared to 42% statewide in 1987.

LOIS LENSKI COVEY FOUNDATION

Please describe your library facilities and staff:

When funds for the library at Missouri Valley College were
given to the college in the 1920's, it was with the
understanding that the library would also be open to the
residents of Marshall. This arrangement never proved
satisfactory as the college necessarily geared its
collection to the courses being taught. In addition, it was
usually closed during the summer and on spring and Christmas
breaks.

A small group of people worked for many years to get a
public library. They were finally successful and on March
19, 1990, the first public library opened in Marshall. The
City of Marshall provided the library with facilities on the
basement level of the new Municipal Building. All shelving
and the circulation desk were purchased at a nominal cost
from the Mid-Continent Public Library in Independence.

The majority of the opening day collection consisted of
donated books. The library is funded with a 20 cents per
$100 valuation tax. In addition, the Missouri State Library
provided a start-up grant. The collection has grown to
20,000 volumes in one year.

Patrons of the library are served by an automated catalog
and circulation system. Through the ability to retrieve
items using only key words, the collection can be used to
its fullest extent. A CD-ROM machine allows access to the
holdings of all major libraries in Missouri. Interlibrary
loans are requested through the computer, via a special
hook-up with the American Library Association.

The library was one of 20 public libraries in the country
chosen for a Voices and Visions demonstration grant. This
grant is funding a poetry discussion series and includes the
honorarium for a scholar, videotapes, anthologies, and
brochures.

LOIS LENSKI COVEY FOUNDATION

Programs have been diverse and well-attended. Pre-school story hours are held twice a week, one in the morning and one in the afternoon. Each story hour has a theme. There is also a special program planned each month for Kindergarten through second grade; third and fourth grades; and fifth through eighth.

Monthly circulation averages over 4000 volumes. This is phenomenal considering the fact that there are only 20000 books to be circulated. There is no bookstore in Marshall and the community's people have been starved for books for a long time.

The staff consists of the Library Director and four part-time employees. The Director has a Master's Degree in Library Science from the University of Missouri and 23 years experience in school, special, and public libraries. Two of the part-time employees also have Master's Degrees in Library Science from Central Missouri State University. The children's leader has a Bachelor of Science in Education and Art. The fourth employee has a Bachelor of Science in Education.

Staff training and continuing education are a priority. The Library Director is active in the American Library Association and attends annual and mid-winter conferences regularly. The children's leader just returned from a day-long Children's Literature Festival at a nearby university. The Assistant to the Director attended a week-long summer institute sponsored by the Missouri State Library.

Please give us any additional information you feel would be useful to our directors.

Because children in Grades 3, 4, 5, and 6, are in a crucial stage of their reading development, we believe that the public library must provide a large variety of fine children's literature selected especially for them. They have learned to read and often read voraciously. Since we are such a new library, we have been unable to meet this demand.

There are 784 children in Grades 3 through 6 in Marshall. Approximately 49% of these students are eligible to receive free or reduced school lunches. Because of the changing family structure and the depressed economy, over one-half are considered to be "at risk".

In addition to providing a strong children's collection for this age group, we propose to offer a program series called the "Newbery Celebration: The Best of The Best." This would be a nine month celebration and include a special program for parents in observance of the second anniversary of the Marshall Public Library.

Children will participate in the library for at least two hours each week. A different Newbery award winner will be highlighted each month. The first month will be devoted to

LOIS LENSKI COVEY FOUNDATION

<u>Strawberry Girl</u> and the children will vote on the remaining 8 books. Activities each week will be interdisciplinary and structured to include a game, a craft, food, and information. Following is the format for Lois Lenski's <u>Strawberry Girl.</u>

Information

o   Find all the information you can about Lois Lenski - in the encyclopedia, <u>Junior Book of Authors</u>, <u>Something About the Author...For Young People</u>, and other reference books.

o   Find a picture of Lois Lenski.

o   There will be questions and answers about Lois Lenski. One child will pretend to be Lenski while the other is an interviewer. They will ask the questions and answer them in front of the group.

o   Use visuals to show grapevine swing; high top shoes; cypress swamp; cow and mule chips and home composting; and grasshoppers and the damage they can do to the land.

o   Discuss what it would be like without a school; the Florida backwoods and accents; what it would be like if you had no mirrors and could only see your reflection in a lake.

o   Define "dinner buckets", "crackers", "yard-plays".

Games

o   Gopher Turtle Races. Turtles will be in a circular box which has half moons cut out at intervals around the bottom. Each turtle has a number on its back. The box is lifted and the first turtle to cross the line is the winner.

o   Gameboard with letters. Each child must fill out something for each letter. It does not have to be a complete sentence but must have happened in the book.

    Example:

    S   Slater's don't want neighbors.
    T   Tater's (sweet) were given to babies to satisfy
         them.
    R   Racing was part of "Yard Games".
    A   Alligator blocked the road.
    W   Wire fences angered some people.
    B   Bunny sat on ant hills.
    E   Every Sunday the Boyers went to church
    R   Roddenberry Place is where the Boyers moved.

o   Cut out shapes of strawberries. Write questions about the books on one side and answers on the back. Meant just for fun!

Food

o   Eat fresh strawberries

o   Make strawberry "fruit leather"

LOIS LENSKI COVEY FOUNDATION

o   Make strawberry sugarplums. Dip a marshmallow into warm milk. Take the marshmallow out of the milk with a toothpick or tongs and drop it into a container holding strawberry Jell-o. Cover the jar and shake until the marshmallow is thoroughly coated.

o   Strawberry no-bake (condensed milk, strawberry jell-o, vanilla, sugar, and coconut.

o   Have a taffy pull, as in the book.

o   Each child will bring a strawberry recipe from home and compile a "Strawberry Girl Cookbook".

Crafts

o   Hats (Birdie gets a new bonnet). Using paper plates, with ribbon pulled through slits on either side to tie under the chin. Each child will decorate as he or she wishes.

o   Design your own brand. "Our markin's on the cow"

o   Make dollies from towels.

o   Make clothespin dolls of favorite characters in the book

o   Make dioramas or paintings or drawings of favorite scenes.

At the special program for parents, during the library's birthday celebration, children will dress as their favorite character from Strawberry Girl and read excerpts from the book. They will also distribute their cookbooks and display their crafts.

BUDGET	Library	Grant
Children's leader 72 hrs. with children 216 hrs preparation @$5/hr	$1440	
Materials including publicity fliers, etc.	$540	
Newbery paperbacks for each child participating		$900
500 titles selected for age group from Children's Catalog		$6000
TOTAL	$1980	$6900

SELECT BIBLIOGRAPHY

Note: See also the list of resources on pages 69 and 70.

PLANNING/MARKETING

Jacob, M.E.L. *Strategic Planning: A How-To-Do-It Manual for Librarians.* New York: Neal-Schuman Publishers, Inc., 1990.

Kies, C. *Marketing and Public Relations for Libraries.* Metuchen, N.J.: Scarecrow Press, 1987.

Kotler, P. *Marketing for Nonprofit Organizations.* 2nd ed. Englewood Cliffs, N.J.: Prentice-Hall, 1982.

Lubow, A. "The Studio 54 of Culture," in *Vanity Fair* (May 1986): 110-114, 133.

McClure, C. R., et al. *A Planning and Role Setting Manual for Public Libraries.* Chicago: American Library Association, 1987.

Palmour, V., M. Bellassai, and N. DeWrath. *A Planning Process for Public Libraries.* Chicago: American Library Association, 1980.

Walters, Suzanne. *Marketing: A How-To-Do-It Manual for Librarians.* New York: Neal-Schuman Publishers, Inc., 1992.

GRANT SEEKING

Boss, Richard W. *Grant Money and How to Get It: A Handbook for Librarians.* New York: R. R. Bowker Co., 1980.

Corry, Emmett. *Grants for Libraries.* 2nd ed. Littleton, Colo.: Libraries Unlimited, 1986.

Grants for Libraries and Information Services. COMSEARCH Broad Topics Series, no. 26. New York: Foundation Center, 1990.

Grants Thesaurus. Phoenix, Ariz.: Oryx Press, 1986.

Hall, Mary. *Getting Funded: A Complete Guide to Proposal Writing.* 3rd ed. Portland, Oreg.: Continuing Education Publications, 1988.

Kiritz, Norton J. *Program Planning and Proposal Writing.* Expanded version. Los Angeles: Grantsmanship Center, 1980.

Libraries Getting into the Philanthropic Thick of Things. Washington, D.C.: Taft Group, 1988.

Margolin, Judith B., editor. *The Foundation Center's User-Friendly Guide, Grantseekers Guide to Resources.* New York: The Foundation Center, 1990.

National Society of Fund Raising Executives, Foundation Center, and American Library Association, comps. *Money, Money, Money for Libraries, Libraries, Libraries: A Fund Raising Bibliography.* Alexandria, Va.: National Society of Fund Raising Executives, 1988.

Swan, James. *Fundraising for the Small Public Library: A How-to-Do-It Manual for Librarians.* New York: Neal-Schuman Publishers, 1990.

Weaver, Shari L. *Federal Grants for Library and Information Services: A Selective Guide.* Chicago: American Library Association, 1988.

Woolls, Blanche. *Grant Proposal Writing: A Handbook for School Library Media Specialists.* Westport, Conn.: Greenwood Press, 1986.

JOURNALS OF INTEREST FOR GRANT SEEKING

The Chronicle of Philanthropy. 1225 23rd Street, N.W., Washington D.C. 20037. Biweekly.

Foundation News. Council on Foundations, Inc., 1828 L Street, N.W., Suite 300, Washington, D.C. 20036.

Grants Magazine. Plenum Publishing Corporation, 233 Spring Street, New York, N.Y. 10013. Quarterly.

INDEX

Peggy Barber is Associate Executive Director for Communications of the American Library Association in Chicago.

Linda Crowe is Director of Peninsula and South Bay Cooperative Library Systems in San Mateo, California.

Book design: Gloria Brown
Cover design: Apicella Design
Typography: C. Roberts